MW00616970

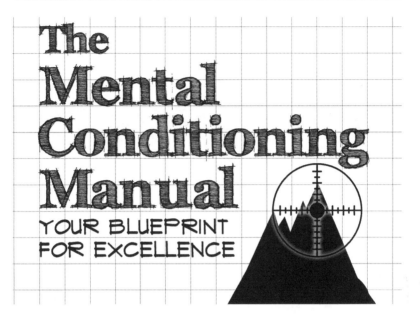

The Mental Conditioning Manual

YOUR BLUEPRINT FOR EXCELLENCE

This manual is being given to

_____

because I care about you and your journey up

The Mountain of Excellence

BRIAN M. CAIN, MS, CMAA

Brian Cain Peak Performance, LLC

What Champions Are Saying About Brian Cain
& *The Mental Conditioning Manual*

"This manual is the foundation of our mental conditioning program. Cain keeps simplifying the process and making it easier to train the six inches between the ears that control the six feet below. This is a must-have for any coach or player."

Vann Stuedeman, Head Softball Coach
Mississippi State University

"I take this with me when I leave the house for spring training. It has everything I need to keep me focused on the process and what I need to do to play my best."

Andrew Cashner, San Diego Padres, Pitcher
2008 1st Round Pick, Chicago Cubs

"Cain is the Master of the Mental Game. He helps you to keep yourself focused on the right things to help your performance. The Mental Conditioning Manual is a key part of my routine."

Bryan Holaday, Detroit Tigers, Catcher
2010 Johnny Bench Award for Top Catcher in College Baseball

"Playing the game one pitch at a time is a critical part of success in baseball. Living your life one pitch at a time is also the best way to accomplish your goals off the field. What I love most about The Mental Conditioning Manual is the amount of information you can get in one place. For high school and college coaches and athletes, this manual is a must."

Frank Pecora, Head Baseball Coach
Northfield High School,
Vermont State Champions
77, 83, 84, 85, 88, 89, 90, 97, 98, 99, 00, 01, 06, 07, 12

"This is your blueprint for excellence. You do not need to waste your time reading anything else. If you use this manual, you will become a champion."

Jeff Guilmette, University of Vermont Hall of Fame
8X America East Conference Shot Put Champion

"Brian Cain has 'IT,' the ability to reduce a lot of important information into manageable 'sound bites.' He provides coaches and athletes with a 'toolbox' of mental/emotional skills to help them perform in competition."

Tom House, PhD
Former Major League Baseball Pitcher and Pitching Coach

"Cain gives you a system for communicating and teaching more effectively about competitiveness, mental toughness and the skills athletes need to succeed in college football and in life. His program made a huge difference in our 2010 Big South championship season."

David Bennett, Former Head Football Coach
Coastal Carolina University, 2010 Big South Champions

"Brian Cain was a big part of helping us develop a system for coaching and developing mental toughness. We have had him on campus to work with our team and staff and do Skype calls with him throughout the season. It has made a HUGE difference for our program."

Dina Graves, Head Girls Soccer Coach
The Woodlands High School
The Woodlands, Texas, 2010 Texas 5A State Champions

"If you are serious about championship level performance and are willing to put in the work it takes to be successful, this is exactly the manual you need to take it to the next level. Cain's program is the best in the game, by far."

Andrew See, Assistant Baseball Coach
Duke University

"Never before has a manual been put together that has everything you need in one place. His system gives you EVERYTHING you need to make mental conditioning as simple and effective as possible."

Casey Weathers, Professional Baseball Pitcher
2007 1st Round Pick, 8th Overall, Colorado Rockies,
2008 Olympic Bronze Medal

"The secrets of success are in your hands. The Mental Conditioning Manual is a breakthrough in peak performance and personal development. This is your blueprint for making excellence a lifestyle, not an event."

Jim Schlossnagle, Head Baseball Coach, TCU
2004 - 2012 Conference Champions
2010 Men's College World Series
2010 National College Baseball Coach of The Year
2013 USA Baseball Collegiate National Team Field Manager

"Brian Cain's Mental Conditioning Manual is the blueprint you need to train mentally just like you train physically for performance. This book is a career changer and will take your performance to the next level."

Tom Brands, Head Wrestling Coach, The University of Iowa
NCAA National Champions '08, '09, '10
National Wrestling Hall of Fame
1996 Olympic Gold Medalist, Freestyle Wrestling 136.5lbs
4 x NCAA All-American, 3 X NCAA National Champion

If this manual has had a positive impact on your career and you would like to have a testimonial featured in future editions of *The Mental Conditioning Manual*, please e-mail us at Testimonials@BrianCain.com. We look forward to hearing how this manual has positively affected your game and your life. We look forward to working with you to become a master of the mental game, and to helping you DOMINATE the day.

In Excellence, Your Mental Conditioning Coach

Brian Cain

The Mental Conditioning Manual
YOUR BLUEPRINT FOR EXCELLENCE

BRIAN M. CAIN, MS, CMAA

Brian Cain Peak Performance, LLC
www.BrianCain.com

www.MentalConditioningManual.com/extras
**For BONUS Mental Conditioning Material &
FREE Peak Performance Training Tools**

Peak Performance Publishing

Brian M. Cain, MS, CMAA
Mental Conditioning Coach
Peak Performance Publishing
Brian Cain Peak Performance, LLC

The Mental Conditioning Manual:
Your Blueprint For Excellence
A Masters of the Mental Game Series Manual

Printed in the United States of America
Edited by: Jackson Penfield-Cyr, Justin Dedman
Cover design & manual layout: David Brizendine
Illustrations: Nicole Ludwig and Greg Pajala
Photography: Don Whipple and Paul Lamontangue
Publisher's Catalog-in-Publication
(provided by Quality Books, Inc.)

Brian M. Cain, MS, CMAA
The Mental Conditioning Manual:
Your Blueprint For Excellence
A Masters of the Mental Game Series Manual

Library of Congress Control Number: 2012950980
ISBN: 978-0-9830379-6-5

PREFACE

The Mental Conditioning Manual: Your Blueprint For Excellence is the third works in the *Masters of the Mental Game Series.* This manual is an extensive collection of works that, when put into action, will change your career and change your life.

This is a manual on excellence and its attainment through personal and group achievement. The aim of this manual is to provide you with the guiding principles that will give you the best chance for success in anything you do.

As you work to be excellent in sport, it is important to appreciate that the principles of excellence are applicable to all aspects of life. If it is worth doing at all, it is worth doing to the best of your ability. The principles of excellence have universal application.

This is a manual for people looking for simple yet effective ways to improve their performance. This manual will not delve into theory or research, but is itself a body of research in which you are able to learn from my experience on what works in the field of mental conditioning, self help and peak performance.

The material in this manual has worked for real people in real programs. Whether you are a veteran of mental conditioning or just getting started, this manual will provide insight and information you can use to help unlock your potential. Let this manual serve as your blueprint for excellence.

Compete in the moment and live in the big picture.
    –DOMINATE THE DAY!

DEDICATION

This manual is dedicated to you. Because you are committed to excellence, you have chosen to invest the time it takes to be different, abnormal and uncommon, and to take your performance and your life to the next level.

By signing your name below you are dedicating yourself to this manual and to the journey up The Mountain of Excellence. This text is your mountain guide, and by reading it you will discover who you are, what you truly desire, how to excel in your athletic career, and more importantly, in your life.

I _____ (print your name) have been given everything I need to become excellent. I am fully capable of living the life of my dreams and leaving this world a better, more excellent place.

I am devoting myself to the pursuit of excellence. I realize that this journey has no finish line and that there is no single summit to The Mountain of Excellence. Different goals represent different summits, but my approach to the journey must be consistent and exceptional in order to accomplish every climb.

I am committing to the creation of a positive legacy. I realize that the legacy I leave will be defined by what I do today, because it is the sum of my todays that constitute my career and my life.

I realize that my legacy will be further defined by the relationships I develop and how I treat my teammates in life. Therefore, I am hereby committed to improving the relationships in my life and my greater community by improving myself.

Every day, in an attempt to become the person I desire to be, I will wake up and make the inspired commitment to improve myself and take steps to get closer to my dreams.

I realize that I will not be as excellent each day as I want to be, and not as excellent as I am going to be, but I will work every day to make progress and to be more excellent than I was the day before.

I hereby sign my name below to certify my commitment to the pursuit of excellence!

_____

ACKNOWLEDGMENTS

It is with sincere and deep appreciation that I acknowledge the support and guidance of the following people who helped make this manual possible.

Special thanks to John T. Allen, Dan Nolan, Adam Batista, Bruce Brown, Dr. Rob Gilbert, Ed Agresta, Harvey Dorfman, Lou Pavlovich Jr., Jonathan Cardozo, Dr. Ken Ravizza, Meghan Turcot, Tom Simon, David Brizendine, Jackson Penfield-Cyr, Justin Dedman, and the thousands of coaches and athletes who have shared their stories and have influenced the writing of this manual.

www.MentalConditioningManual.com/extras
For BONUS Mental Conditioning Material &
FREE Peak Performance Training Tools

CONTENTS

FOREWORD

This is a manual about excellence - excellence in sport and, more importantly, excellence in life. If you have this manual in your hands, it is my goal that this manual becomes "that book" – the book that changes your life.

This manual contains the principles and lessons I have learned and taught over my career as a mental conditioning and peak performance coach. In most ways, this manual is the product of my experiences throughout this great learning process, and represents the accumulation of the knowledge I have gained and wish to impart to those who strive for daily excellence.

Being in the dugout during the NCAA College World Series in Omaha, working as a mental conditioning coach with NCAA Champions, cornering Ultimate Fighting Championship World Champions in Main Event bouts in Las Vegas, working with athletes competing for their home country in the Olympic Games and working with coaches and athletes in Major League Baseball, the National Football League, the National Hockey League and in the National Basketball Association as a mental conditioning coach, are just a few of the standout moments I have been fortunate to experience in my career. I am humbled by the privilege I have to live the life of my dreams, and I move forward in life with an attitude of gratitude. I understand, however, this privilege is not guaranteed to me, and my success is the result of my unwavering commitment to excellence in my career and to having the opportunity to surround myself with successful and selfless people who have shown me the way.

This manual will reveal the philosophy and processes I use to accomplish everything. From owning my own business to being a #1 best-selling author, it has been turning the failures and adversity in my life (there have been a LOT) into learning experiences that make me stronger.

I, by no means have it all figured out. I fail a lot more than I succeed and have as many challenges in my life as anyone else. But what I have figured out is how to embrace life's challenges and see them as at-bats in life's great game and as an opportunity to improve my game. Either way, I have learned to say "So What, Next Pitch!" Flush the mental bricks, take the fish hook out of my mouth, and move on.

Human growth and development happen through experience - the experience of the events in your community, the people you meet, the programs you watch, the music you listen to, and the books you read. It is my sincere hope and desire that using this manual becomes a life-changing experience for you.

AUTHOR'S NOTE

The intent of the author in writing this manual in the *Masters of the Mental Game Series* was to create a comprehensive mental conditioning manual that could be used by athletes and coaches as their blueprint for excellence. *The Mental Conditioning Manual: Your Blueprint For Excellence* outlines the Peak Performance System of PRIDE (Personal Responsibility In Daily Excellence).

The PRIDE program consists of 15 elements of mental conditioning that are essential to the practice of performance excellence. A chapter is devoted to each of the 15 elements, which may be covered in order or by specific topic. The mental conditioning techniques within each chapter will affect every individual differently, but the mental conditioning skills they address are all significant to mastering the mental game.

Mental conditioning and peak performance is all about searching within yourself to see what you are made of as a performer. When you search within yourself, you learn that all the answers to life's questions and challenges live inside you. As you work your way through this manual, you will learn what compels you to embark on this self-transformative journey of self-improvement by continuously reflecting upon yourself.

While reading about each element of excellence, you will recognize the mental adjustments and changes you must make to access all the untapped and limitless potential that resides inside you. Tapping into every ounce of combined mental and physical potential is the art of peak performers and this manual will teach you this art form by coaching you to search from within.

The photo above has impacted me since I first saw it in 2002 and illustratively captures the concept of one's ability to search within oneself. My life's mission is to help you uncover the excellence that lies within you and to coach you to develop the tools necessary to achieve performance excellence by looking inside.

www.*MentalConditioningManual.com/extras*
For BONUS Mental Conditioning Material
& FREE Peak Performance Training Tools

CHAPTER #1

INTRODUCTION TO PEAK PERFORMANCE
AND MENTAL CONDITIONING

What is peak performance? What does it mean to be at your best when it means the most? What is mental conditioning and why is it essential to both understanding and answering those two questions?

This is your mental conditioning manual – a manual that will give you the knowledge and techniques to unlock all of your performance potential. The coaches and athletes I have worked with at national championship-winning college programs; state and national championship-winning high school programs; the Olympic Games; Ultimate Fighting Championship; National Football League; National Hockey League; National Basketball Association; and Major League Baseball have all experienced one thing in common: as you elevate to higher levels of competition, success becomes less about the physical skills and more about mental skills.

This truth is essential to acknowledging and appreciating the importance of mental conditioning, and the more you think about it, the more obvious it becomes. At the highest levels of competition, everyone has the physical skills to be successful or else they would not be competing at that level. Talent is simply just not enough. If it was, every 1st round pick in the Major League Baseball Draft would make it to the Major Leagues. Thus, on top of developing the physical skills to compete at the highest level, athletes must devote more time to the development of the mental skills that will allow them to perform consistently at an elevated level above their athletic peers. It is no secret that the best performers on the planet are masters of the mental game.

To further emphasize the significance of mastering the mental game, there is a simple two-word sentence to convey the significance of mental conditioning to peak performance: *consistency wins.*

Consistency is the significant difference between the good and the truly great performers. Those who perform their craft at the highest level on a consistent basis are the legendary and iconic figures in their respective sports. Anyone who has the physical prowess necessary to compete has the ability to perform at the highest levels of their sport once in a while, but it is the warrior athlete who brings his best every time he performs that will make the biggest impact on his team, in his sport and will ultimately have the greatest career.

WHAT MAKES THE BEST OF THE BEST

Demanding the best possible performance from your body is a characteristic of all great athletes. However, physical development to your peak potential does not come cheap. The most competitive athletes invest significant amounts of time and energy into the many grueling hours it takes to train their bodies for performance at the highest levels of their sport.

The greatest athletes in any sport are aware of something that everyone else might not be. It is the simple fact that if you want to be the best of the best, doing the physical training is simply not enough. They know that mental conditioning is essential for them to develop a psychological edge over their greatest competitors and give their physical preparation the necessary direction during athletic performance. The greatest competitors understand that peak performance occurs only when the body and the mind are working together to maximize their performance potential. Thus, the best of the best know that mental conditioning is as vital to their success as physical conditioning.

THE POWER OF THE MIND

The power of the mind is as miraculous as it is incomprehensible. Studies have continued for years and we are still miles away from truly understanding the full capabilities of the human brain. Countless examples of "mind-over-matter-type" experiences have been documented over time. There are incredible examples of prisoners of war being released and performing amazing physical feats having practiced mental conditioning during their detentions.

One such example is of a POW who came out of exile having visualized playing golf every day so that by the time he was free and stepped onto a golf course he lowered his golf game by ten strokes. Upon his release, another POW who practiced mental conditioning, became a competent guitarist by teaching himself the guitar through repetitive visualization processes, despite never playing the instrument before. There are endless, miraculous stories similar to these, and it is safe to say that even though neurological function is not as well understood as the physiological, no one is prepared to discount the human mind as the most powerful tool available to mankind.

The good news is that even without understanding the

scientific intricacies of the human mind, anyone can improve their mental toughness with a simple mental conditioning program and by doing simple yet profound techniques and exercises. This is what this mental conditioning manual is all about.

MENTAL CONDITIONING

Mental conditioning is the process of psychological modification by which an individual exercises and develops influence over his mental state in order to control his behavior. When divided between the two words, *mental* is of or relating to the mind, while *conditioning* means to train or accustom oneself to behave in a certain way or to accept certain circumstances. To mentally condition oneself in regard to a particular stimulus means to literally make one mental response to that stimulus firm, solid, and real in one's mind.

Most people do not initially identify thoughts as solid entities, but the process of internalizing thoughts with perceived value through mental repetition creates firm and solid beliefs reflected in the individual's perception of reality. This is the result of mentally conditioning your subconscious, a process similar to an individual physically conditioning his body in the weight room. When you lift weights infrequently, you do not seem to get any stronger, but when you lift weights consistently, the timely repetition will make you stronger. Mental conditioning gives you the techniques to develop control over the beliefs in your mind.

Beliefs both positive and negative shape our behavior, create our experiences, and determine our results. Philosophers and spiritual leaders have been preaching the power of beliefs for centuries, while scientists have been conducting research on how the mind works for decades. Professional athletes, however, were among the first in our culture to recognize the practical application of positive affirmation training and the implications of mental conditioning for their performance. They realized that, by integrating positive confidence conditioning statements and mental imagery into their daily training regimens, they could improve their performance reliably, and often dramatically. The goal of this manual is to give you the tools to develop your mental game to shatter limiting beliefs and develop the confidence conducive to performance excellence.

HAVING A MENTAL CONDITIONING SYSTEM

It is an unfortunate reality that most athletic programs leave mental toughness to chance. Many coaches think that their players will either figure it out or they won't; that their players either have it together between the ears or they do not. These coaches believe there is nothing they as the coach can do to help enhance the athlete's mental toughness other than tough physical conditioning. However, performing at your best when it means the most is as much about the six inches between your ears as it is the six feet below them.

This coaching mentality fails to recognize that developing a strong mental game has just as much, if not more, significant value to performance than developing a strong physical game. The mental game skills of having a present moment focus and positive perspective on the process and performance preparation, along with the discipline and dedication to your sport and personal goals, regardless of adversity and the failures you face, are all skills that can be taught, developed, and continuously improved. Mental conditioning is strength and conditioning for the six inches between your ears that control the six feet below them. Having a mental conditioning system is paramount to peak performance excellence and it will give you a skill set to be successful in sport and, more importantly, successful in life.

THE 90% / 10% SHIFT

Whether or not coaches and athletes understand the complete significance of mental conditioning, most coaches and athletes I have worked with will initially agree that training for competition is 90% physical and 10% mental. They acknowledge that when game time rolls around a noticeable shift occurs. In the heat of competition they concede that performance becomes 90% mental and 10% physical. This is called the 90%/10% shift to give athletes and coaches an illustrative taste of how valuable mental conditioning is when it is time to perform.

The reality, however, is that there should be no shift. Mental conditioning should be integrated into physical conditioning and every aspect of performance preparation. It should be 100% mental and physical conditioning combined, because one is never complete without the other. This mental conditioning manual will give you a system along with the tools for conditioning your mental game. As you read this manual and develop your mental toughness, think about it as going to the gym to do strength and conditioning for your brain instead of your body. Then when you go to the gym, practice the techniques and philosophy you have learned. This is the process to becoming a peak performer.

YOUR BLUEPRINT FOR EXCELLENCE

I always get the question, "Brian, when you work with professional athletes, college programs, or high schools, what do you teach?" What I teach is a mental conditioning program that will allow you to play your best when it means the most, by teaching you how to:

- Live in the present moment and maximize your time.

- Act different than how you feel and start having good "bad" days.

- Focus on the process over the outcome.

- Identify what you can control and what you cannot.

- Have your own personal philosophy and core values for life.

- Challenge your limiting beliefs and your perspective.

- Stay positive in the face of adversity.

- Develop preparation and performance routines for consistently, high level performance.

- Take responsibility for your performance and life.

- Relax, recover, and gain control of your thoughts, feelings, and emotions.

- Recognize your signal lights and develop the awareness to win.

- Release negative thoughts and refocus back to the present when you get distracted.

- Move from intelligence and thinking to action and results.

- Use mental imagery to help you prepare and be more confident in your performance.

- Inspire and motivate yourself to make the impossible possible.

- Develop the dedication and self-discipline that you need to power through the grind it takes to succeed.

- Take action steps to make excellence a lifestyle, not an event.

These are the fundamentals of mental toughness and represent the blueprint for an athlete to take personal responsibility in daily excellence. Through learning, understanding, and using this mental conditioning manual, your mind can successfully direct your body to achieve the level of excellence necessary for peak performance.

CHAPTER #1 REVIEW

- Consistency wins.

- If you want to be the best of the best, doing the physical conditioning is not enough. You must do both physical and mental conditioning.

- Peak performance occurs only when the body and the mind are working together to maximize their performance potential.

- The power of the mind is as miraculous as it is incomprehensible.

- Mental conditioning is the process of psychological modification by which an individual exercises and develops influence over their mental state in order to control their behavior.

- Mental toughness is taught, developed, and continuously improved upon.

- Mental conditioning should be integrated into physical conditioning and every aspect of performance. You do not separate the mental and physical conditioning; you do them together.

NOTES:

NOTES:

_____

_____

_____

_____

_____

_____

_____

_____

_____

_____

_____

_____

_____

_____

_____

_____

_____

_____

_____

_____

_____

_____

_____

_____

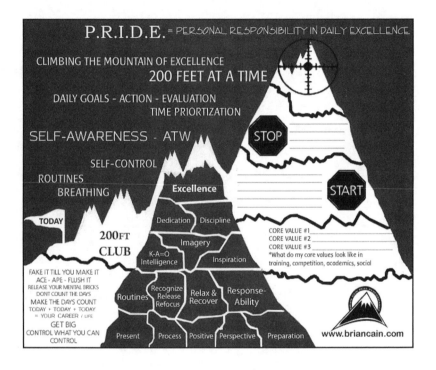

CHAPTER #2

P.R.I.D.E. AND THE MOUNTAIN OF EXCELLENCE

When you look at people who are truly excellent performers and high-level achievers in athletics, academics, business, and/or life in general, there are essential mental principles that are consistent across the board. This manual provides you with a blueprint for adopting these fundamental principles and applying them to your sport and life.

This blueprint is provided to you in the form of the PRIDE program, a system for mental conditioning I created stressing 15 essential elements of excellence. PRIDE is an acronym for Personal Responsibility In Daily Excellence. This acronym serves as the backbone of this mental conditioning system, reminding you of the significance in making excellence a daily pursuit for which you are personally responsible.

Performance excellence is the ultimate achievement of any peak performance athlete and is what this manual will assist you in accomplishing. But, before you can become a peak performer, you must first understand *excellence* in performance. It is defined as follows:

Excellence is being at your best when it means the most – every single day.

For a baseball player, being your best when it means the most is every single pitch. In football, it means every single down. In hockey, it means every single shift. In basketball it is every possession and in mixed martial arts, it is every time you step into the cage. If you are a student, it is every single class. Regardless of your performance arena, taking PRIDE is the establishment of an overall system for success. It is absolutely necessary to help achieve an elite and excellent performance state of mind and body.

THE MOUNTAIN OF EXCELLENCE

The Mountain of Excellence is a symbolic concept used throughout this manual. The summit of the mountain represents your goal while the mountain represents the obstacle one must conquer to reach it. The journey up The Mountain of Excellence marks the self-transformative endeavor an individual must take to become a peak performer.

This manual employs the concept of The Mountain of Excellence while addressing the 15 elements of excellence in the PRIDE Program to demonstrate that the achievement of performance excellence is a long, but worthwhile journey. Similar to mountain climbing, peak performance is about training to achieve an excellent climb up one mountain. Once that mountain is conquered, it is time to return to base camp and set your sights on the next mountain's summit.

Mountain climbing also serves as a great activity to compare with sports achievement. When an individual or team scales a mountain, they cannot simply live on the summit: they must return to base camp and either perform the climb again or find another mountain. Similarly in sports, an individual or team cannot win a championship and be champions forevermore. They will forever be champions of that season, but as soon as the next season rolls around, the slate is swept clean and all the opposition is ready to become title contenders. This forces the champions to start the season anew in their quest for that season's championship. The achievement of reaching the summit therefore is only temporary.

Ultimately, there is no end to the pursuit of excellence; no one final summit to reach. Peak performance is a constant journey pursuing excellence and demanding personal responsibility in this daily pursuit. As you read this manual, the use of the mountain climbing analogy and understanding the peak performance concepts embedded within it will assist your perception of the mental game as you strive to transform yourself into a peak performer.

WHAT IS YOUR SUMMIT?

In reading this manual, it is clear that your immediate Mountain of Excellence is conquering this manual to understand how to achieve performance excellence and transform yourself into a peak performer. However, it is only by fully understanding the reasons for embarking on this journey and openly recognizing the larger mountain you desire to conquer, that you will make the most of your self-transformative experience. Therefore, you must begin with the end in mind to give your journey a greater sense of purpose. You must know precisely where it is you want to end up and why you want to end up there, or you might find yourself climbing the wrong mountain.

Think about your desired destination. Is being the best mental conditioning coach in the world the top of your mountain? Is it winning a state or national championship? Winning a World Series? Breaking a particular record? Getting into the college of your choice? Landing that million dollar deal, or simply making the team? Whatever your journey, you must begin with the end in mind. You must have an outcome goal and a destination.

 ACTION STEP: What is The Mountain of Excellence you desire to climb and conquer? What is it you want to accomplish?

8/7/14 - Full Ride to UAB

_____

_____

_____

_____

_____

 **CAIN'S COACHING POINT:**
Remember, you are allowed to climb more than one mountain, but should focus on one summit at a time. Keeping your mind in the present moment, sticking with the process and staying positive will help you to better enjoy your journey and experience more success than if you mountain hop and pursue different summits during the day. Whatever mountain you are climbing at that time, focus on that specific summit. Be where you need to be when you need to be there and hike one step at a time.

THREE-STEP PROCESS TO ACCOMPLISHING ANYTHING

Most people have heard the saying "You can do anything if you set your mind to it" but are skeptical of deeming it a universal truth. Well, I am one of those people who believe that if you truly desire something, why not set your mind to it and give everything you've got to achieve it. To make your dreams become a reality you must pursue your goals in an effective and realistic manner. This is why peak performers must understand and effectively utilize the three-step process to accomplishing anything, both in sports and in life.

The three steps that give you the best chance to accomplish anything are:

1. Make a commitment to your goal by writing it down and putting it where you can see it on a daily basis.

2. Make it public and share your goal with your teammates, friends, family, accountability partners, and the people in your inner circle.

3. Work with a relentlessly positive energy on a daily basis to make it happen – the type of relentlessly positive energy that can only be found when you are pursuing something you are passionate about and have a reason why. So be very selective about your goals.

These three steps provide you with the strategy that gives you the best opportunity to accomplish anything you desire.

As you proceed on your journey through this manual, utilize these steps to accomplish your process-based goals along the way. This is why you identified and established your mountain in the previous section to facilitate the first step of this process and your personal journey. It is your job to facilitate step number two, and it is the purpose of this manual to provide the information and knowledge to facilitate step number three so that you may conquer the mountain and reach its summit.

ONE DAY (TODAY) AT A TIME

Now that you have established your mountain and know the three principle steps to reaching the summit, it may still appear to be an intimidating mountain to climb. Do not be daunted by your destination. You chose it because you want it: because a fiery passion within you burns and yearns to shed its light on the snow-capped pinnacle of your mountain. You will conquer your Mountain of Excellence, but all in good time. As we all know, patience is a virtue.

There is a flag in the bottom left corner of The Mountain of Excellence image. The flag is labeled "Today." It says "Today" because that is where we are – every day.

Each morning when you wake up, a new climb up The Mountain of Excellence begins. In your backpack are your experiences and what you have learned on previous journeys from past days. Make your journey by focusing on one day at a time.

The importance of taking one day at a time cannot be overstated. You know your desired destination – the Summit of Excellence – but you must familiarize and condition yourself with the fundamental principles necessary for survival. This must be done on a daily basis.

As any mountain climber preparing to ascend Mount Everest, one must gradually build the stamina and conditioning for the long trek to the summit. Putting in the time and establishing mental endurance is of paramount importance, so that you are prepared for the treacherous conditions you are bound to face on your long journey. Practicing what you need to succeed one day at a time will get you to your summit.

CORE VALUES

As you set your sights on the summit of The Mountain of Excellence, you must begin to prepare for your journey by establishing core values. A core value is a personal belief and virtue reinforced through a commitment to yourself and your teammates. You must identify your personal and organizational core values in order to realize what you stand for both now and for the future. These core values will provide an internal guide to direct you on your journey and will reflect how you approach your pursuit of excellence.

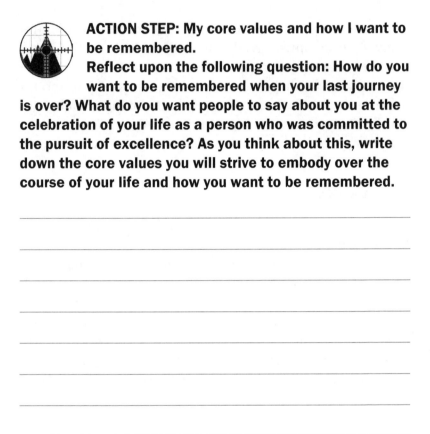

ACTION STEP: My core values and how I want to be remembered.
Reflect upon the following question: How do you want to be remembered when your last journey is over? What do you want people to say about you at the celebration of your life as a person who was committed to the pursuit of excellence? As you think about this, write down the core values you will strive to embody over the course of your life and how you want to be remembered.

_____

_____

_____

_____

_____

_____

_____

CAIN'S COACHING POINT:
Answering the question of how you want to be remembered when your life's journey is complete will help provide clarity to what is most significant to you and how you will want to begin living your life today.

As you reflect upon this big question, consider how your core values transfer to your sport. Think about how you would like people to acknowledge you and your contributions to that sport and your team over the duration of the current season.

The reason we transition focus to a set of core values for the present (off-season into the season or vice versa) and not for an entire lifetime is that a lifetime is a daunting time frame. A lifetime is too difficult to imagine and therefore presents an intimidating mountain to climb. It is important to focus on how you want to live over the course of the season in order to focus on how you must live in the present moment. Establishing this perspective will make climbing your mountain appear much more manageable.

Once you have identified what you want people to say about you and you have reflected this in your core values, start living by them "Today." These core values are fundamental principles that should be integrated into the routines of your daily life. If you are not regularly practicing these principles, you will end up losing your way to the summit.

APPLYING CORE VALUES TO LIFE

When you look to the future, you may think it is difficult to have integrity for your entire life, or to be responsible for your entire life or to have self-discipline for your entire life. This may be true, but you CAN live with integrity, responsibility and self-discipline "Today." With this perspective, you have an appropriately-sized mountain to climb "Today." And then, do it all over again when tomorrow becomes "Today."

To begin applying core values to your sport and life, choose one or two and focus on them for a set period of time.

CAIN'S COACHING POINT:
I recommend working on your specific core values for 4-5 weeks. Research shows it takes 21-28 days for positive personal change to occur with a focused plan and accountability partner. Right now, look over your core values and ask yourself, "how do I apply my core values in my life at this present time?"

Imagine it is the month of December and one of your core values for December is being self-disciplined. As you commit yourself to working on your self-discipline this month, think about the following:

How would I define self-discipline?

What does self-discipline look like in the different aspects of my life?

If I am an athlete or a coach, what does self-discipline look like in competition, in training, in academics, at the nutritional table, in recovery, and in my personal life?

To provide myself a point of reference and to give me a chance at living that way, how do I identify specifically what it is to be self-disciplined in those areas?

Answering all of these questions is significant to defining exactly what it is and how it is you plan on living this core value. If you specifically outline your core values, you give yourself the best opportunity to live them.

By establishing what it looks like for you to live your core values, you set yourself up for success. *It is easier to act your way into thinking and feeling than it is to think and feel your way into action.* Knowing what action you must take and how you will take it to become the new-and-improved version of yourself sets the stage for a successful journey.

When establishing your core values I suggest you focus on between one and three for a given period of time. Initially, setting more than three would be an overwhelming endeavor. Giving yourself a more narrowed focus will increase your chances for successful mastery of a particular core value. If you can focus on self-discipline for the month of December, you are going to have the skill of self-discipline beyond December into January.

SUCCESS LEAVE CLUES

Here is some insight into achieving a successful career in anything you do: *success leaves clues.* If you want to be a millionaire, go hang out with people who are millionaires. If you hang out with people who are making $50,000 a year and you tell them you want to make a million dollars a year, what are they going to do? They are going to laugh at you, because they do not see it as a reality. But, if you go hang around people who make a million dollars a year, you are going to get some ideas as to how to make your first million.

The same rationale is true for sports. You always hear coaches telling players, "If you want to get better, play with people who are better than you." This is because when you play with better players, you begin to pick up the clues to their success. Imitation and adaptation to higher levels of competition will ultimately lead to performance improvement and success of your own.

SURROUND YOURSELF WITH BETTER STUDENTS

To further illustrate the importance of hanging out with the right crowd, I will share a personal story from high school. When I was a high school student, I was not great academically. But, then I reached a point where I knew I needed to improve my grades to play college baseball. I made a self-improving adjustment in my life and began surrounding myself with those who were academically more successful. I am an example of will over skill.

In pursuit of my goal, I started going to the library with more successful students to study. I didn't feel like going to the library, but I went anyway. These students had a pre-established discipline that I knew I needed to develop.

I began noticing their study habits. I started to learn that there are techniques you can use that are very simple to help with memorization and knowledge acquisition. I began to imitate them, and I started to get better results.

Success is largely about discovering a winning formula and implementing the system that facilitates excellence. Mastering the mental game is no different. If you surround yourself with those devoted to performance excellence, your chances of achieving it will drastically improve. When you invest your time properly to a winning system in the pursuit of excellence, success will take care of itself.

DAILY GOAL-SETTING & TIME PRIORITIZATION

Beyond the establishment of core values, daily goal-setting and time prioritization are important for establishing the routine discipline necessary for peak performance. I used to call it time management, but have since learned that you will manage your time based on how you prioritize your time; therefore, *time prioritization is one step before time management.*

CAIN COACHING POINT:
There is only ONE factor among everyone in the world who is competing for what you want. You all have only 86,400 seconds in a day. Most will spend time, you will INVEST time. If you are not efficient with your time, the competitors who are will pass you by. Learn to take control and advantage of your time, or your time will take control and advantage of you.

With time prioritization in mind, you must take advantage of your time or time is going to take advantage of you. As an aspiring peak performer, you must find different ways to make the best investment of your time to accomplish the daily goals you set.

Throughout this manual, I will share with you techniques you can use to better invest your time. For example, a great technique for time prioritization is to write down what you want to accomplish the next day on your bathroom mirror with a dry erase marker. I started doing this and have found it to be an effective technique because you are in your bathroom frequently throughout the day and the writing on your mirror will remind you constantly of what you need to accomplish. It also provides an effective method of preparing for the next day. When you go to bed, you will be relaxed knowing you have already got a jump-start on the new day. By simply preparing the night before, your daily goals will always be waiting for you on your mirror when you wake up.

THREE STEPS OF PERFORMANCE CHANGE

Whether it is practicing core values or prioritizing your time, peak performance is all about continuous personal development and necessary change. Championship-winning coaches and athletes know that they must first become champions of personal responsibility in daily excellence before winning championships. They also know this takes an understanding of how to make necessary adjustments to change their performance to attain successful results.

One of the most successful mental conditioning coaches I have ever met was Harvey Dorfman, author of *The Mental Game of Baseball* and mental conditioning coach to some of the greatest athletes in the world. Having spent some time with Harvey, he taught me that, if you want to make a performance change, there are three essential steps you must follow:

1. Develop an awareness of what needs to change.

2. Develop a strategy for change.

3. Implement the strategy with an accountability partner and assess yourself regularly so that the necessary performance change can occur.

Most athletes fall short of significant performance improvement because they either lack the awareness of what they need to change, do not formulate an effective strategy for the change, fail to facilitate the strategy to bring about the necessary change, or have a "YES" partner not an accountability partner. Without this three-step system of performance change, an athlete can never achieve the necessary performance improvement to achieve excellence.

Here's a prime example of the three steps of performance change:

I was working with a pitcher who was 20 pounds overweight. I had the pitcher wear a 20 pound backpack to help develop his awareness of what it felt like to be 20 pounds over weight, but also what it would feel like to lose the extra 20 pounds he was carrying.

He wore the backpack around campus all day and at the end of the day came back to see me. He took off the pack and said he was exhausted. We went to throw a bullpen session just like he had done in the morning with the pack on, but this time the pack was off. After throwing, I asked how it felt throwing without the pack on compared to how it felt throwing with the pack on. He said it was like night and day.

I placed my hands on his shoulders looked him in the eyes, and said, "When you shed that 20 pounds you told me you wanted to lose, you are going to feel this good every day. Think about how much better you are going to be." This is a prime example of INSTANT AWARENESS.

This athlete went through an experience that immediately conveyed an awareness he would not have had otherwise. This experience demonstrated that, "When I lose the weight, I am going to feel like I do, right now, without that pack on." There is the awareness. Then, we came up with a strategy for him to lose the weight. He contacted a sports nutritionist, approached his strength and conditioning coach about his goals, and together they developed a strategy for him to lose that excess weight.

Notice that the athlete did two things: made his goal public and established strategies with multiple accountability partners, to assure implementation. Only you can make the necessary improvements; nobody else can make your performance change. It is absolutely essential that you hold yourself accountable to your goals, and the best method is making your goals public. As one of his accountability partners, I talked to him once a week. After a number of months, he dropped the 20 pounds, became a much better pitcher, was stronger physically and mentally, and realized that with the right strategy and system he could accomplish anything. *SO CAN YOU.*

As exhibited through this example, the change begins with an awareness of what needs to change. Once this is accomplished, a strategy must be developed for the change. Finally, the accomplishment of positive change for performance improvement begins to manifest through the implementation of the developed strategy and consistent assessment with your accountability partners. The three-step process to accomplishing anything combined with the three steps of performance change provides you with the fundamental mental conditioning tools to effectively and successfully utilize the material within this manual.

SELF-ASSESSMENT: STOP – START – CONTINUE

In order to further initiate your personal development and facilitate the accomplishment of your goals, you must assess yourself to build self-awareness. As an aspiring peak performer, you must assess your most recent performances to establish self-awareness of what you must improve in your pursuit of excellence. Take a look at your last three days. What are some actions or behaviors that you are doing that you need to STOP in order to achieve the goals that you have set?

 ACTION STEP: What I must STOP doing in order to achieve my goals:

1)_____

2)_____

3)_____

Now, I want you to write down what it is you must START doing to help you achieve your goals.

ACTION STEP: What I must START doing in order to achieve my goals:

1)_____

2)_____

3)_____

Now, I want you to write down what it is you must CONTINUE doing to help you achieve your goals.

ACTION STEP: What I must CONTINUE doing in order to achieve my goals:

1)_____

2)_____

3)_____

The Stop, Start, and Continue activity is a very simple process that ought to be frequently practiced to provide self-assessment and to keep you moving up your mountain. It is a simple activity to keep yourself honest about your work effort, but it is often not performed enough.

SIMPLE vs. EASY

It is here that I will take a moment to address an important distinction in both mental conditioning and performance in general. For any performer, it is important to be cognizant of a very significant distinction between the words "simple" and "easy." Simple and easy are not synonymous. Just because something is simple in concept does not mean it is going to be easy to do. If all simple things were easy, everyone would perform them and everyone would be successful. There would be no reason to strive for performance excellence.

Unfortunately, that is just not the reality, and this is why this manual is aimed at the pursuit of excellence. There are a lot of average people walking around who have excellence buried inside of them but are not trained or not willing to harness their hidden potential. As you read this manual, you must consistently work to adopt and implement the simple practices and techniques that make a significant difference in performance.

THE NEXT 200 FEET

Imagine you were to hike from base camp to the top of The Mountain of Excellence - the tallest mountain in the world. If you were to leave base camp at midnight, could you hike to the top of The Mountain of Excellence on the trail that takes you to the summit? The answer is a definitive "Yes." It will be dark out, but you have the ability to hike the entire way up the mountain in complete darkness because of your head lamp. Your head lamp allows you to travel anywhere in the dark, because it illuminates the next 200 feet of the path. Therefore, by simply focusing on the next 200 feet, it is possible to hike through the darkness to the summit.

When you are hiking the next 200 feet, animals may attack you. You might take a wrong turn, you may challenge Sasquatch with some beef jerky, and/or you may roll an ankle. These events symbolize the adversity you are sure to face on your journey, and they are all outside your control. All you can do is embrace the adversity and do what is necessary to reach your destination.

When metaphorically hiking up the mountain, the biggest obstacle we face is our obsession with the end result, the destination. This destination disease is representative of whatever end result you desire – e.g. the championship, the starting line-up, a particular stat line, the perfect season, or the Hall of Fame. Remember that the *destination is the disease and the journey is the reward.*

Excessive focus and time devoted to looking at the destination beyond the next 200 feet is a common illness. People set their goals too far out in front of them without understanding, creating, and implementing a process to get there. By focusing on the outcome, people become stationary dreamers as opposed to advancing toward their goal, 200 feet at a time. This is, quite simply, inaction versus action: the dichotomy between thinkers and doers. This is the condition of people counting down the days until that dream comes true as opposed to making the days count in a proactive and productive pursuit of that dream. A dream without action will remain a dream, while a dream that motivates action has the opportunity to become a reality.

As you proceed through each chapter of this manual, remember to focus on the next 200 feet as opposed to the summit of your mountain. This will prevent you from being overwhelmed at times and make the ascent appear more manageable. Keep the process over the outcome and the journey over the destination.

REFUSE THE URGE TO BE AVERAGE

As you start to apply the strategies in the mental conditioning manual to your life, you will receive some criticism and some people may make fun of you for your commitment to self-improvement and performance excellence. Do not listen to the voices of negativity for they are the voices of the masses – they are the voices of the average.

Average people and average teams are the best of the worst and the worst of the best. Do not settle for average; strive for excellence and set your sights on the summit. Reach the pinnacle of success by climbing The Mountain of Excellence with a focused determination on your goals with a dedication to personal responsibility in your daily excellence. Hike that next 200 feet and you will learn that there are no traffic jams on the extra mile.

START YOUR JOURNEY

The rest of this manual is devoted to the 15 elements of excellence within the PRIDE program. The material within these chapters will give you the mental conditioning skills to establish your blueprint for excellence. View each chapter as if it is the next 200 feet and conquer the mountain that is this manual. It is a journey that will provide you with the knowledge and skills to make the progress necessary to reach the summit of your mountain.

Remember, the internalization of the peak performance philosophy produces your self-transformation. It is the experience accrued from actively practicing the mental conditioning material within this manual that will ultimately enable you to reach the summit of your Mountain of Excellence.

It has been said that it is the start that stops most people. So do not wait. Get started, RIGHT NOW!

Remember, if you take out the four middle-letters out of "Do<u>N'T WA</u>it!" you get "DO IT!"

So don't wait, DO IT! Get started on your journey up The Mountain of Excellence, TODAY!

CHAPTER #2 REVIEW

- PRIDE = Personal Responsibility In Daily Excellence

- Excellence is being at your best when it means the most – every single day.

- The Mountain of Excellence represents the obstacle one must conquer to reach his outcome goal at the summit.

- The journey up The Mountain of Excellence is a self-transformative endeavor an individual must take to become a peak performer.

- One cannot live at the summit, you have to keep hiking or you will die.

- There is no end to the pursuit of excellence.

- Peak performance is a constant journey pursuing excellence and demanding personal responsibility is this daily pursuit.

- Choose your Mountain of Excellence you desire to climb and conquer.

- Remember, you are allowed to climb more than one mountain, but should focus on one summit at a time.

- The Three Steps to Accomplishing Anything
    1) commitment to a goal
    2) make it public with an accountability partner
    3) work with a relentlessly positive energy today

- Today is where we are, every day.

- A core value is a personal belief and virtue reinforced through a commitment to yourself and your team.

- Live your core values.

- It is easier to act your way into thinking and feeling than it is to think and feel your way into action.

- Success leaves clues.

- Surround yourself with those who are better than you.

- Take advantage of your time or time is going to take advantage of you.

- The Three Steps of Performance Change
    1) awareness
    2) strategy
    3) implementation

- Frequent self-assessment is essential to establish performance awareness.

- Simple and easy are not synonymous.

- Focus on the next 200 feet of the task at hand.

- A dream without action will remain a dream, while a dream that motivates action has the opportunity to become a reality.

- Do not settle for average, it is the best of the worst and worst of the best.

- It is the start that stops most people, so get started TODAY!

NOTES:

_____

_____

_____

_____

_____

_____

_____

_____

_____

_____

_____

_____

_____

_____

_____

_____

_____

_____

_____

_____

_____

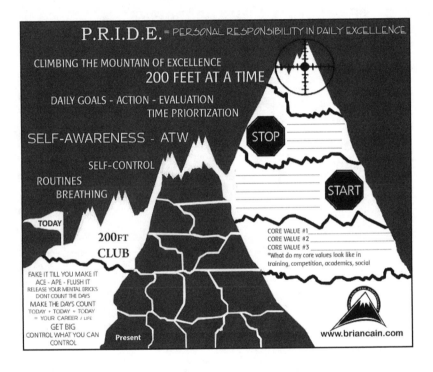

CHAPTER #3

Yesterday is history, tomorrow is a mystery, and today is a gift—that is why we call it the present.

The time is now and the place is here. One of the biggest challenges in life and in becoming a master of your mental game is developing an appreciation for the value in the present and then effectively possessing the ability to channel your performance focus into it. This mission focuses on the present, the first of the Five P's of the PRIDE program. In this chapter you will develop an appreciation for the importance of the present and you will learn how to develop your present moment focus.

In the previous mission you learned about the mindset of peak performances and started to identify your values and put your focus on the plan as to how you will summit your mountain. You learned the importance of concentration on the next 200 feet and the process it takes to climb to the summit. As a committed athlete and someone who wants to develop their mental toughness, you must understand that you *do not count the days, you make the days count.* But how do we actually make the days count? The first step is possession of a present moment focus.

THE 30-SECOND DRILL

Before discussing the present, I want you to experience it. In the following exercise, I want you to live in the present moment by immersing yourself in a present moment focus. Taught to me by my mentor, Ken Ravizza it is called the 30-second drill.

Now as you read this, I want you to invest 30 seconds of your time as if your life depended on what you were reading. Sit up straight in your chair with your feet flat on the floor. Now, I want you to look at each word and hear it as if I am there inside your head speaking to you.

I want you to read every word with a commitment that if you could regurgitate what it is you just read, you would win a million dollars. Think of it as the million dollar mentality, because when you focus with this type of intent all the time, it will not be long before someone wants to pay you a million dollars to work for them.

Ready?

Give me 30 seconds.

GO!

For a short period of time you can do anything you want with your levels of attention, energy, and focus. Right now, the focus you are reading with is different than it was 10 seconds ago – feel that.

You see, you are more locked in right now than you were 15 seconds ago – recognize that. You are currently demonstrating your ability to be into the present moment.

If you can focus like this without someone having to ask you, that is the manifestation of present moment mental toughness. So, while you read this mission over the course of the next 10 minutes, I want you to come back to this level of focus as many times as you can and lock in for 30 seconds at a time.

That is 30 seconds. You are allowed to space out for a moment.

Whew... I hope you felt the intensity of those 30 seconds.

If I asked you for 10 minutes of total undivided attention with that level of focus, you'd probably say, "Cain, that is crazy. There is no way I can read with that intensity for 10 minutes." Challenge yourself to become immersed in the present, and when you get distracted or space out, recognize that you are distracted. Then release and refocus back into the present.

When you think of the present moment focus, compare it to watching a sports performance. For example, if you have ever been to a large baseball stadium, and you go to the top row and watch the game, there is a pulse. As the pitcher begins his motion, everybody steps into the present. Ball one. Everybody steps out.

There is a pulse to the game. There is a routine ebb and flow to the game, where the performers, and even the audience, enter the present, play the pitch, and exit that moment after the play occurs. It is a short, intense focus followed by a space-out. That process repeats itself over and over about 300 pitches a game. Essentially, it is a much shorter version of the 30-second drill the players use as a part of their routine to get into the present moment.

As you read this chapter, you will develop an enhanced understanding as well as the mental skills of present moment focus. What is important to remember is that you can get here, the present moment, anytime you want. It is all a matter of awareness and choice.

IN vs. INTO

On your path to understanding the present moment, there is an important distinction that must be addressed. Peak performers recognize there is a substantial difference between the mindset of being "in" versus being "into" your performance. As you are reading this section, I want you to experience the difference between being in and being into the present moment by asking yourself the following questions:

Are you reading this manual because someone wanted you to or are you reading this because you want to be a peak performer? As you read, are you highlighting or underlining text you feel is important? Are you taking notes in the margins? Are you fully engaged in the process or are you just in? Are you into or just in?

People who possess an in-mentality, who go through the motions or are doing things because other people want them to or because they feel like they "have to" only last for so long before being replaced by people who possess "into" mentality. Those who are truly "into" are driven by a purpose. Being "into" means you are doing something because you want to and you are passionate about your performance because you want to be at your very best.

As you elevate to higher and higher levels of competition, talent means less and less because everyone has talent. Everyone in Major League Baseball has talent. Everyone in the Ultimate Fighting Championship has knockout power. Everyone at the highest level of any sport has the talent to win on any given night if their opponent does not compete to the best of their ability. Pride yourself on being into the day-to-day grind of doing what must be done to be successful and on being "into" the journey up The Mountain of Excellence versus just being "in" for results.

HOCUS-POCUS or FOCUS-REFOCUS

Realize that success in any endeavor is not the product of hocus-pocus. You are not going to be successful today because the moon and the sun and the stars and the galaxy just happen to line up for you. You are going to be successful to the degree that you are able to focus, and refocus when you become distracted.

Success is not hocus-pocus magic: it is actually much simpler than that. Success is largely dictated by your ability to maintain present moment focus on the tasks at hand. The key to developing an intense and productive focus is to recognize when you become distracted, take a deep breath, and then refocus your attention.

You will get distracted, because everyone does. The attainment of peak performance is contingent on the development of distraction awareness. You must develop the ability to recognize when you are distracted and then refocus back into the moment. An easy way to remember this is to think, if I want to win, I must focus on *What's Important Now (WIN)*. Focus on what you are doing right here in this moment and to accomplishing the tasks in the present moment. This is the focus of performance excellence and successful progress.

WATCH OUT FOR FISH HOOKS

Through recognizing that we all get distracted from time to time, it is equally important to recognize what distracts us.

The term "fish hooks" is symbolic of the negative thoughts from external stimuli that your mind can get caught on during your pursuit of excellence.

 For a FREE chapter from Cain's #1 Bestseller, *Toilets, Bricks, Fish Hook and PRIDE: The Peak Performance Toolbox EXPOSED,* **please visit www.ToiletsBricksFishHooksAndPride.com/extras to learn more about how you can use the fish hooks analogy in your life and with your team.**

Fish hooks represent distractions beyond your control that you focus on, which deplete your energy and rips you away from performing your best and living in the present. Examples of fish hooks could be obnoxious fans, poor officiating, unprofessional coaches, irritating teammates, past mistakes, etc., all of which are outside of your control.

Ultimately, fish hooks are a hassle and a needless waste of your time. You must develop an awareness of them so you do not get hooked, and so that when you do, you can get off the gaff before getting ripped out of the water.

To further illustrate the application of fish hooks in performance, think of yourself as a fish. As a fish, you are swimming in a school up Performance River to the destination of Lake Excellence.

As you swim upstream, you need sustenance for your journey, so you dine on whatever you can find. You discover worms are an especially delicious but rare treat. You have observed some of your friends try to eat worms dangling in the water only to get stuck in the mouth with a fish hook.

You learn you must be wary of fish hooks when you see a worm. If you accurately identify fish hooks with worms, you can actually still have a meal by eating around the hook. Thus, if you keep the presence of mind to inspect your worms carefully, then you will give yourself the best chance to reach Lake Excellence.

In this analogy, the worms are the opportunities to learn and succeed on your journey to performance excellence and the fish hooks are the external stimuli within those opportunities that could keep you from your forward progress. As a performer (or fish), you must stay in the present moment and strategically seize the opportunities for self-improvement.

You must focus on what you can control – your presence of mind – and work around the fish hooks that have the potential to hold you back. If you see the worm but forget to check for a fish hook, then you are bound to get hooked.

Be aware of fish hooks. Do not get hooked.

ACTION STEP: I want you to identify three fish hooks that you deal with on your team. What distractions have a tendency to deplete your focus and get you hooked?

FISHHOOK #1 _____

_____

FISHHOOK #2 _____

_____

FISHHOOK #3 _____

_____

USING CONCENTRATION GRIDS:

Concentration grids have been a staple of mental conditioning for years. This game/exercise is all about concentration and efficiency, which is best accomplished by staying in the present moment. Concentration grids are a great way to increase your ability to stay in the present moment for an extended period of time.

Your training program with concentration grids is simple. Cross out the grid numbers from 00-99, in order, as fast as you can. During this exercise, you are testing yourself to see how efficiently you can perform the task. You are also testing your ability to concentrate and stay in the present.

Start practicing this exercise in a quiet environment to become comfortable with the activity and to monitor your present moment focus. Once you have become proficient at it in a quiet environment, you may play music or do this activity in front of the TV as a way to include distractions just as there will be when you compete. The more you do this activity and the more quickly you can cross out the numbers in order, the more you are developing your ability to concentrate and keeping your mind in the present moment.

Athletes I have worked with report that the grids allow them to become more aware of when they start to space out and lose focus, when they slip out of the present and into the past or the future. The exercises also allow them to become more aware of when they are trying too hard and need to take a breath in order to relax and get back into an optimal level of focus.

It is also important to keep track of the time it takes to complete each grid. When I started doing concentration grids on a routine basis (Monday, Tuesday, Thursday, and Friday mornings before I ate breakfast), my time was in the low- to mid-teens in minutes. After almost two months, I was able to do them in about four or five minutes, even in the crazy and chaotic environment known as a high-school cafeteria.

Here are some sample concentration grids you can use to help train yourself to stay in the present moment for an extended period of time.

 Get 50 Free Concentration Grids at www.MentalConditioningManual.com/extras

Brian Cain Peak Performance, LLC
Concentration Training Grid
www.briancain.com
www.briancaininnercircle.com

64	12	20	15	69	80	31	57	95	61
71	63	05	73	07	36	38	91	83	58
39	01	53	42	62	35	43	04	59	89
34	78	09	70	97	72	24	87	88	40
44	47	67	27	85	41	16	77	74	84
54	55	76	93	92	10	98	48	45	00
33	66	46	49	21	75	94	18	52	14
81	82	06	28	68	08	23	60	11	99
02	03	86	37	25	30	26	50	22	17
51	79	13	65	56	96	90	29	32	19

Brian Cain Peak Performance, LLC
Concentration Training Grid
www.briancain.com
www.briancaininnercircle.com

64	12	20	15	69	80	31	57	95	61
71	63	05	73	07	36	38	91	83	58
39	01	53	42	62	35	43	04	59	89
34	78	09	70	97	72	24	87	88	40
44	47	67	27	85	41	16	77	74	84
54	55	76	93	92	10	98	48	45	00
33	66	46	49	21	75	94	18	52	14
81	82	06	28	68	08	23	60	11	99
02	03	86	37	25	30	26	50	22	17
51	79	13	65	56	96	90	29	32	19

ROUTINES MAKE THE DIFFERENCE

Developing performance routines is essential to mental focus on the present moment. Mission 8 is devoted to the significance of performance routines, but you should always be developing, establishing, and improving your own routines.

One of the best examples of how developing performance routines keeps you in the present moment happened at the 1973 figure skating world championships. Russian pair figure skaters Irina Rodnina and Alexander Zaitsev had their music unexpectedly stop during their free program. The two partners, however, were so engrossed in the present moment of competition that this adversity did not faze them, as, without missing a beat, the pair successfully completed their program in silence. Upon the program's completion, spectators responded to the performance with a thunderous standing ovation. This memorable performance earned them the gold medal in these world championships and their performance remains a testament to the power of present moment focus.

Imagine being that connected to what you are doing; so immersed in the present that when your music shuts off, you are as cool as an ice rink. The skaters performed as if they didn't even notice their music stopped because they were so intensely focused on the present moment and concentrated on the successful execution of their routine.

In my work with figure skaters, we will often have them imagining themselves going through their skating routine. It is amazing how in-sync the pair can be even when sitting on the floor with their eyes closed independent of each other. They get so into the routine and so into the moment, they cannot be distracted.

As you read this manual reflect upon the new and different material you are exposed to regarding peak performance. With your newfound awareness of specific material, strategize and develop methods to integrate the material into your daily routines, and then implement them. Remember the three steps of performance change, for this is how you will become proficient in the present.

INVEST YOUR 86,400 SECONDS

We all have 86,400 seconds in a day. Everyone also has a choice of whether they want to spend that time or invest it. If you spend your time, it is gone. If you invest your time, you get a return in the future. Thus, by investing time, you are making the educational decision to maximize the benefits of the time you are given. Choosing to apply time toward learning from those who are better than you in any particular area in which you seek improvement, will ultimately give you a big return.

The investment of time in the present will give you the greatest return on your time. *The time is now and the place is here.* Performance excellence is about performing tasks in your sport with greater efficiency and effectiveness, and developing a superior present moment focus is crucial for this to happen. As you move forward in this manual, begin practicing methods, such as the 30-second drill, deep breathing, concentration grids, and other techniques to help maintain a present moment focus. Similar to climbing a mountain and using the 30-second drill, it is all about focusing on the present moment and taking one step at a time until you reach the summit of The Mountain of Excellence. Investing time is the philosophy embedded in the PRIDE program, and in the essence of the present.

CAIN'S COACHING POINT:
Yesterday is a cancelled check, tomorrow is a promissory note, and today is cash: invest it wisely.

CHAPTER #3 REVIEW

• Yesterday is history, tomorrow is a mystery, and today is a gift—that is why we call it the present.

• Do not count the days, make the days count.

• The present moment is a matter of awareness and choice.

• Be "into" the present moment as opposed to "in" it.

• Success in athletics is not hocus-pocus. It is all about your ability to focus and re-focus.

• Focus on WIN (What's Important Now).

• Beware of fish hooks.

• Train your present moment focus by using concentration grids.

• Establish present moment focus routines.

• Invest your 86,400 seconds and get a big return.

• The time is now and the place is here.

NOTES:

NOTES:

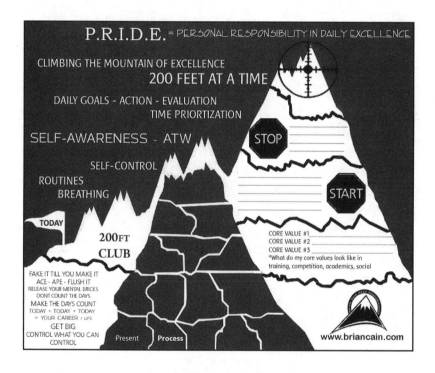

CHAPTER #4

PROCESS OVER OUTCOME

The ability to perform at a level of excellence on a consistent basis is the goal of all peak performers. As the previous chapter discussed, the maintenance of a present moment focus will assist you in this goal; however, you must have something to focus on in the present moment during performance. This something is the process.

A peak performer's focus must always be on the process. By keeping focus on the present elements of the performance process, athletes give themselves the best opportunity to perform on the level of excellence. An excellent process will yield excellent results, and performing a step-by-step process directed at excellence will get you up the mountain. Remember, the commitment and concentration on the next 200 feet of the hike will get you safely to your destination. Focus on being excellent on your journey step-by-step up The Mountain of Excellence and you will be sure to reach the summit. This climb demands a peak performer.

UNLEARN WHAT YOU HAVE LEARNED

The society we live in is a results-driven society. If you are a coach reading this, you will not likely have a job if you do not win games. The kicker is that to win games you must not focus on winning, but on the process of winning. Coaches and athletes I work with most often unlearn what they have learned to focus on in their sport – mainly winning and focusing on other outcomes that are outside of their control vs. processes that are within their control and that give them the best chance for success.

A peak performer must understand that winning is the outcome of performance excellence; thus, the product of an individual's or team's performance. The focus of the individual athlete and team, therefore, ought to be their performance, because that is what is truly within their control and yields the desired outcome. More precisely, a performer's focus should be on the process of his performance to provide the best opportunity for his performance excellence.

CAIN'S COACHING POINT:
You must often unlearn what you have learned and realize that what got you here, might not get you there. You must always be asking yourself, is this the best way?

THE LAW OF AVERAGE

Former Louisiana State University head baseball coach, Skip Bertman won five national championships in 1991, 1993, 1996, 1997 and 2000. A true Master of The Mental Game, Skip stressed the importance of the process and emphasized that anytime you play baseball (or any sport) there are only four possible occurrences:

1. You can play well and win.

2. You can play well and lose.

3. You can play lousy and win.

4. You can play lousy and lose.

Coach Bertman called these the law of average because if you play your best, you give yourself the best chance to win – BUT you are not guaranteed to win. What he knew was that he never had control over the outcome of the game. All he had control over was how prepared his team was come game day and then how they played. Through this understanding of the game, Coach Bertman knew that the process of performing excellently was what won games, not a focus on winning games. As a coach, he made the law of average swing in his favor by emphasizing the process of performance excellence over the outcome of winning. You can swing the law of average in your favor as well, if you commit yourself to the process.

THE BEST TEAM NEVER WINS

I have had the wonderful privilege of getting to know and work with Ultimate Fighting Championship Welterweight Champion, Georges St. Pierre. Georges is one of the best athletes on the planet and a large part of his consistent success has been his ability to stay focused on the process of becoming the best fighter he can be (the journey) while letting go of his desired outcome to be and maintain the status of world champion (the destination).

By focusing on the process of being the best he can be through constantly evolving as he aims for self-improvement and personal progress, Georges gives himself the best chance to retain his World Championship title. Georges realizes that even though he is one of the best fighters, if not the best fighter, on the planet, he can get knocked off the summit of mixed martial arts on any given night. He has learned the hard way that the best fighter never wins. It is always the guy who fights the best.

Visit www.MentalCondtioningManual.com/extras to see an interview between Georges St. Pierre and Brian Cain after St. Pierre's victory at UFC 74 in which they break down the mental approach for success inside the Octagon.

"I truly believe that I am the best fighter in the world. And, in every sport it is the same story. It is not the best team that wins in baseball; it is the team that plays the best. It is not the fastest horse who will win the race; it is the horse who races the best. And Saturday night, even though I believe that I am the best fighter in the world, Saturday night the guy who's going to win the fight is the guy that will fight the best. I am very glad to fight Josh Koscheck. He's the number one guy right now after the title holder, so I want to get back to what I lost and I go step by step. I am very happy to fight him."

Georges St. Pierre
Ultimate Fighting Championship Welterweight Champion
2008, 2009, 2010 Canadian Athlete of the Year
UFC 74 Pre-Fight Press Conference

This quote is from Georges on the eve of his UFC 74 fight with Josh Koscheck, his first fight after losing his World Championship to Matt Serra at UFC 69 on April 7, 2007. I love what he says about how the best fighter never wins, it is always the one who fights the best. I hope you can see that he clearly understands the value of the process.

CAIN COACHING POINT:
St. Pierre saying "I go step by step" illustrates the mentality and focus on the process as well. When he says "I am the best fighter in the world," he displays his confidence in his abilities, but he recognizes that "the guy who's going to win the fight is the guy who will fight the best." This truly emphasizes his mental ability to separate the outcome from what he must do to achieve it.

The same logic can be applied to any form of competition. You may be the world champion or part of the best team in the world, but during performance it does not matter who is more talented or who has a more impressive resume. In the heat of competition, all that matters is who competes at the higher level. If you are the underdog, and your whole mentality revolves around you playing your game, regardless of the accolades and accomplishments of your opponent, then you have done what I call "released your mental emergency brake," enabling you to play your game at the highest level.

WHY UPSETS HAPPEN

To further challenge and change your perspective on the old cliché that "the best team always wins," let's reflect upon some of the great moments in sports history.

The "Miracle On Ice" in the 1980 Winter Olympics between the Soviet hockey team and the U.S. hockey team. The Soviet team consisted of seasoned professional athletes while the U.S. team consisted of amateur collegiate athletes.

The whole world expected the Soviet team to come out victorious. The Soviets had destroyed the same USA team in an exhibition game 10-3 in Madison Square Garden on February 9, 1980, just days before the Olympics started. We all know, however, the end result was anything but what was expected. The U.S. team's 4-3 victory over the Soviet's will go down in history, undisputedly, as one of the greatest upsets of all time. The better team was clearly the Soviet team, but the team that won was the U.S. team.

Another prime example that defies the "best team always wins" cliché is Super Bowl XLII between the New England Patriots and the New York Giants. The Patriots had accomplished an undefeated season (16-0) and reached the Super Bowl with a cumulative record of 18-0. This Patriots team was hailed by analysts as arguably the greatest NFL team ever and was the 12-1 favorite to be victorious. The victory, however, went to the undaunted Giants who led 17-14 as time expired. Who was the better team? The Patriots. Who played better on that night? The Giants.

Yet another example of a phenomenal upset is the 1985 NCAA Men's Division I Basketball Championship between the Georgetown Hoyas and the Villanova Wildcats. The Georgetown Hoyas were the defending national champions and the No. 1 ranked team in the nation led by Patrick Ewing, the 1984 tournament's Most Outstanding Player and one of the most dominant players in college basketball history. The Wildcats were unranked in the regular season with a 19-10 record and received an at-large bid for a number 8 seed in the tournament. In the National Championship game, Villanova went on to play a near perfect game against a team most thought to be unbeatable. The Wildcats shot an historic 79 percent from the floor as they defeated the Hoyas 66-64 to become the lowest seed in NCAA basketball history to win the national championship. Who was the better team? Georgetown. Who played a better game? Villanova.

In boxing, James "Buster" Douglas, the unknown 42-1 underdog, defeats Mike Tyson; in Olympic wrestling, unknown U.S. wrestler Rulon Gardner defeats Russian wrestler Alexander Karelin, who was previously undefeated in 13 years of international competition; and the list goes on and on. All these upsets are sufficient evidence to conclude that the old cliché "the best team always wins" is false. The main reason is that the more talented teams often get so caught up on the outcome that they forget about the process to achieve what they desire. A huge part of the process is controlling what you can control (your performance) and letting the outcome take care of itself, and when the "best teams" show a mental lapse, the underdog is usually right there ready to seize the moment. We can, thus, definitively state that the best team/athlete never wins; it is always the team/athlete that plays the best.

CONTROL WHAT YOU CAN CONTROL

The peak performance athletes that best understand the significance of the process over the outcome have established proficiency for recognizing what they can control and what they cannot. It is amazing how many athletes still get hung up and hooked on things outside of their control. If you want to become a peak performer, you must learn how to differentiate between what you can control and what you cannot control.

When you put time and energy into things you cannot control, you are wasting both of those valuable resources. Focusing on these things is a self-defeating game and assists the opposition in the process. Peak performers do not play it.

Here is a list of things you cannot control. In sports, you cannot control the officials, the fans, the media, the other team, playing time, the field conditions, the schedule, statistics, batting average, earned run average, coaches, parents and most of all, the outcome of an athletic contest. The only thing you can control is yourself and your APE– your attitude and appearance (body language); your positive self-talk, presence (focus), process (preparation), performance (how hard you compete), perspective and your effort and emotions.

One of my favorite sports I use to illustrate just how little control an individual has while participating in competition is baseball. Baseball and softball are crazy games. You can virtually do everything right and still lose and there are also days where you can do very little right and win. If you are a pitcher on a day when you are placing the ball exactly where you want it over the plate, the hitters may just be connecting with their bats. If you are a hitter on a day when you are connecting on all the pitches you want, the fielders may just be making great plays to prevent you from getting on base, or you may be hitting the ball as hard as you possibly can... right at someone. If you are a fielder, you may make all the right plays to prevent your opponents from scoring, but that one home run the other team hit was the deciding factor on the scoreboard. Baseball and softball are unfair games. So is life. Get used to it, and stop saying "that's not fair." That may get you sympathy when you are in 2nd grade, but not when you are trying to reach the summit.

In baseball and softball, as in life, when you focus on the process of playing the game one pitch at a time and let the outcome take care of itself you will give yourself the best chance for success.

Winning is a by-product of executing the fundamentals and focusing on the process over the outcome. You cannot control winning. If we could control winning, somebody would go undefeated every year because they would figure out what it took to do so and then proceed to do it. In the world of sports, there are just too many variables that you cannot control. Focus on the process and put yourself in a position for excellence, and the process will eventually reward you with success.

WHAT DO YOU CONTROL?

As mentioned above, a huge component of the process is controlling what you can control. In the space provided below, write down all of the things that you can control while performing your sport in the first column and then list the things that you cannot control while performing in your sport in the second column.

ACTION STEP:

CAN CONTROL	CANNOT CONTROL
my attitude	other players
my success	talent
heart, abilities	field conditions
outcome of adversity	umpires
effort, energy,	The pitcher or
How I hit	how fast/slow
How I field.	or where/what
	she throws

Look at the list of things you cannot control. If you choose to focus on these things, you will inevitably beat yourself. If you choose to focus on these things, you are getting hooked. You must keep your focus on what you can control.

APE

As a peak performer, you must focus your attention on what is within your control. External adversity is a part of life: you make the choice of how you react to it. APE provides you with a reminder of just what it is you have the ability to control: yourself.

APE is an acronym to remember that you control:

A - Your attitude and your appearance (body language).

P - Your perspective (how you see things), the process (how you choose to play), your preparation, your presence (focus) and your self-talk (positive).

E - Your effort, your energy, and your emotions.

This acronym is symbolic of the concept "control what you can control." This concept is a fundamental skill of mental conditioning. Self-control is essential to peak performance, and by the end of this manual you will fully understand why it is that you only have control over yourself in the midst of performance. As my mentor Ken Ravizza would say, you have got to be in control of yourself before you can control your performance.

MY GOAL MUST BE IN MY CONTROL

All athletes and coaches will agree that performance goal setting is a critical part of the process in climbing your mountain of excellence. When setting performance goals, you must remember that your goals must be within your control. A common mistake made in performance goal setting is setting performance goals that focus on the desired outcome instead of setting performance goals that reflect the process.

In baseball, a pitcher should not set a performance goal of getting the batter out (outcome), but should instead set a performance goal of throwing a pitch that gives the best chance of getting the hitter out (process). Understand the distinction between focusing on the batter versus the pitch. A pitcher's goal should not be to get batters out; batters get themselves out. A pitcher's goal is to make a pitch appropriate to the batter, the count, and the game time situation, that provides the best chance for the batter to get himself out, when he either swings or does not.

Remember, your performance goal must be within your control. If you are a pitcher, focus on making a pitch, not getting this hitter out. You could make a great pitch and give up a base hit. You should see this as a success because you executed your job, you just did not get your desired result. You can also make a lousy pitch and get an out and you should see this as falling short of success. Even though you got the desired result, your performance was less than excellent because you did not execute the pitch you were trying to throw. You just got lucky. By setting your performance to making quality pitches, you acknowledge and focus on what you can control and give yourself the best opportunity for performance excellence.

By understanding exactly how your game is played – all the real causes and effects of performance within your sport – you can direct your focus to the process of your performance. This knowledge cuts out all the unnecessary elements of the game that most people harp on and gives you a direct route to peak performance. This is what it means to have an understanding of the process when you set performance goals.

CREATING AND USING YOUR PERFORMANCE ABCs

One of the most effective strategies to help you focus on what you can control, and to create an effective process to help you play in the present, is an exercise called Performance ABCs.

Performance ABCs are three keys that can be mental, physical, or a combination of the two that you repeat to yourself, visualize, and think about before and during competition. These ABCs of your performance will keep you focused on the process you need to follow to be successful.

There are many things that athletes may think about at times during performance, from physical mechanics to game strategy, to the opponent, to issues in personal life. Setting ABCs will help keep your mind focused on the proper process for your performance based on the key elements on which you want to focus. This strategy will give you the best chance for success.

Here are some samples of Performance ABCs that I helped create with a top college baseball team. They used this strategy to defeat the #1 ranked team in the country in a two out of three game series.

NAME	*A*	*B*	*C*
PROGRAM	Belief in Self, Teammates, System	Trust the Process, Be Who You Are	Win Pitches
OFFENSE	Quality At-Bats	Be Relentless 1-9	Win Pitches
PITCHING	Own the Island	Attack the Strike Zone	Win Pitches
DEFENSE	Want the Ball	Attack the Ball	Win Pitches
HITTER	Be On Time	Get My Foot Down	Breathe
PITCHER	See Stitch on Glove	Get Arm Out Front	One Pitch At A Time
COACH	Be an Energy Giver	Confident Leader & Positive Body Language	Be Patient & Trust the Process

You can see that we set general Performance ABCs for the program, offense, pitching staff, and defense. We then set individual Performance ABCs for each hitter, pitcher, and coach. Setting Performance ABCs for the program and general positions helps give the team a common focus on the process during competition. It also benefits each athlete and coach to set individual ABCs as a way for them to better identify the individual processes they must follow to give themselves the best chance for success.

I challenge you to create your own Performance ABCs for your sport. Choose categories that apply to your sport and determine an effective set of ABCs that reflect the performance demands of those categories.

 Visit www.MentalCondtioningManual.com/extras for a sample ABCs sheet you can use with your team.

BEST COACHES FOCUS ON THE PROCESS

The best coaches and athletes in the world know the value of focusing on the process. They see the process as a stair case they climb each day. They know what their desired outcome is and focus on that outcome 20% of the time while focusing on TODAY 80% of the time and the steps they must take to get the outcome they desire.

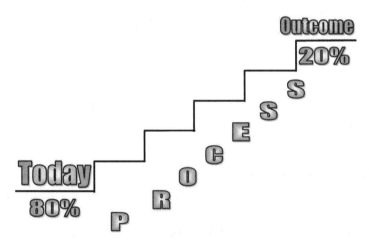

One of the most successful coaches in college football is Nick Saban, who has won the BCS National Championship at LSU in 2003 and at Alabama in 2009 and 2011. Take a look at a quote from his book *How Good Do You Want to Be?*:

"Becoming a champion is not an easy process... It is done by focusing on what it takes to get there and not on getting there."

"It is done by focusing on what it takes to get there and not on getting there" – that is committing yourself to the process.

My challenge for you is to begin committing yourself to the process. Start evaluating your performance on the process it takes to perform at a level of excellence. Focus on the effort you give every day and focus on executing the fundamentals when you perform in practice and during competition. As the swimmer reading this, focus on swimming your race, performing at your best and the mental keys you need to execute versus focusing on beating the swimmer in the lane next to you. As a lacrosse team, focus on playing with great energy and intensity, winning ground balls, and sprinting on and off the field with quick line changes. All the physical mechanics of your sport and all the elements required for the performance of your sport matter, and performing them all excellently is what makes a peak performer.

 ACTION STEP: What are some aspects of the process in your sport that, if you focused on, would give you the best chance to perform at your best?

1. Out front: Hitting and fielding
2. On your toes, read ball off the bat
3. Want and attack the ball

THERE ARE NO LITTLE THINGS

It is worth emphasizing explicitly that there are no little things in the pursuit of excellence. As alluded to in the previous section, one must also recognize and appreciate all the little details of peak performance within your sport to become a peak performer. When you are fully committed to the transformative process of becoming a peak performer, you must be aware of all the details of your performance process, for they are necessary to make a successful journey to the summit of The Mountain of Excellence.

KEEP YOUR LOWS HIGH AND HIGHS LOW

Emotional consistency is essential for excellence. The goal of those striving for success in any arena is to maintain performance excellence day in and day out. The balance of emotions is imperative for consistent peak performance.

When you are faced with adversity and your performance is not reflective of your potential, it is crucial to take a step back from your performance and focus on the process of excellence. Command your emotions by reminding yourself to control what you can control and focus on releasing the mental bricks that can weigh on your mind by having a physical release that you can use, such as clapping your hands or taking a deep breath. *Resist the pressure to personalize performance and remember your work is what you do, not who you are.* By paying attention to the process and not the outcome, you give yourself the best opportunity to achieve excellence, because if you focus on the process and make the necessary changes to it, the result will take care of itself.

The same systematic process is true when you are performing at your best. When you are performing at your highest level and achieving success through performance excellence, it is crucial that you not become complacent. Resist the urge to buy into the hype. Do not think that a little success suddenly renders you more valuable than the process that got you there. Stay humble. Continue to work the process. Give yourself the best opportunity to maintain the excellence you have been achieving by identifying the process you followed to get there and then keep refining that process by making it more efficient and excellent.

On the following page is a "sign of success" from the dugout of the University of Alabama Softball team, the 2012 NCAA Softball National Champions. This image is testament to the program's understanding that you must focus on the process of becoming a champion in order to win championships.

It is challenging to commit oneself to the process of performance excellence. The journey is long and hard, full of obstacles and detours, but this is what makes the glory of achieving performance excellence all the more glorious. Remember, nothing worth having comes easy.

 For more signs of success please visit www.MentalCondtioningManual.com/extras

DEVOTE YOURSELF TO THE PROCESS

Commitment to the process of excellent performance will give you the best opportunity to achieve performance excellence. In this chapter, you have learned that when you devote yourself to the process, you focus on the aspects of performance within your control as opposed to the elements beyond it. You now understand that maintaining control of the process of your pursuit of performance excellence is a means to getting your desired outcome and end result.

Unfortunately, it is common for most people to become fixated on the goal/outcome/end result of performance. As an aspiring peak performer, focus on what you need to do to achieve the outcome and the results you desire. Devoting yourself to the process of performance excellence will undoubtedly give you the best chance to win and, more importantly, reach the summit of The Mountain of Excellence.

 www.MentalConditioningManual.com/extras
For BONUS Mental Conditioning Material & FREE Peak Performance Training Tools

CHAPTER #4 REVIEW

- Unlearn what you have learned about winning.

- Process should always be placed before the outcome.

- Performance Excellence is greater than Winning.

- Know the four possible performance outcomes and the Law of Average.

- The best team never wins. It is always the team that plays the best.

- Control what you can control.

- Develop self-control over your APE.

- Winning is a byproduct of excellent execution of the fundamentals and focusing on the process over the outcome.

- Establish your Performance ABCs.

- "Becoming a champion is not an easy process... It is done by focusing on what it takes to get there and not on getting there." – Coach Nick Saban

- There are no little things.

- Keep your lows high and your highs low – emotional consistency is essential for peak performance.

- Make "signs of success."

- Nothing worth having comes easy.

- When you devote yourself to an excellent process the result will take care of itself.

NOTES:

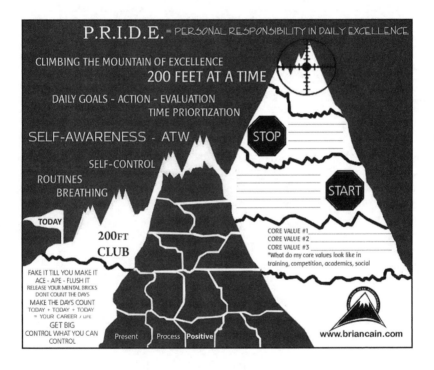

CHAPTER #5

The power of positive self-talk and a positive mentality makes all the difference in an individual's performance. It is a simple concept that is both useful and effective, but is so simple that it is often overlooked. We're used to hearing people tell us to "think positive" prior to performance or in the heat of competition, but the words often roll over our consciousness without our full appreciation of the true value in this all-too-simple piece of advice. Some consider positivity utter nonsense, while others who believe in its power do not understand how to harness this positive mindset to attain their desired results.

Having positive self-talk and a positive mentality is a mental skill that requires proper mental conditioning to utilize its power. The magnificent quality of positivity is that everyone is capable of it. It is simply a mental attitude that is conducive to growth and excellence through the expectation and perception of favorable and beneficial results. This chapter is devoted to conveying the importance of positivity in performance while presenting you with the skills to develop your own positive mentality.

THE PROPHECY OF THOUGHT

The basic tenet is that whatever the mind expects, it will discover. Thoughts manifest through actions and affect outcomes. If you are doubtful you will accomplish a task, you drastically increase the likelihood that your actions and effort will reflect that doubt, and ensure the failure of accomplishment. Similarly, if you possess a positive mentality when faced with a difficult task, you dramatically increase the likelihood that your actions and effort will reflect that positive attitude, and you will succeed.

The successful accomplishment of a task, however, is not guaranteed by positive thoughts. All a positive mentality does is significantly increase the probability that you will walk away from the task, successfully accomplished or not, with greater experience and with greater peace of mind. In this way, a positive mentality makes a significant difference between educational self-improvement and self-stagnation. Thus, your mentality represents the ultimate self-fulfilling prophecy.

THE STORY OF ROGER BANNISTER

On May 6th, 1954, Roger Bannister, a British medical student and avid runner, did the previously unimaginable. From the start of archiving world records and modern time-keeping in track events, no one had been able to break the seemingly impassable barrier of the 4-minute mile. His story demonstrates the prophecy of thought and the power of positive belief.

At the age of 25, the British sports media had already discovered the Bannister, who had become one of the most scrutinized track athletes in the United Kingdom. His speed in the mile and 1500 meter events drew initial attention to his talent, but declining the 1948 Olympics in London to concentrate on his training and his medical studies, he drew the consternation of British track enthusiasts. In 1951, Bannister won the British title in the mile, but his fourth place finish in the 1500 meter race at the 1952 Olympics in Helsinki, the result of a last-minute schedule change that compromised Bannister's preparation routines, fueled further scrutiny for his unconventional training regimen.

After the media publicized his Olympic performance as a failure, Bannister resolved to redeem himself by breaking the seemingly unbreakable 4-minute mile barrier. He increased the intensity of this training, but not the duration, and saw steady improvements in his times, all while he continued to be a full-time medical student. In fact, the duration of his training was less than an hour per day, because he wanted to focus on his study of neurology. Bannister, however, was committed to his new goal and loyal to the process he felt would get him there. He was convinced that as long as he continued to see gradual improvements in his times, he would maintain his own training regimen.

The opportunity Bannister had been training for arrived on May 6, 1954, in a meet between the British Amateur Athletic Association and Oxford University at the Iffley Road Track in Oxford. Running mates Chris Chataway and Chris Brasher exchanged setting the pace for Bannister's first three laps. Bannister unleashed his kick in the last lap, finishing it in less than a minute, before he broke the tape and collapsed in the arms of the gathered crowd at the finish line. The announcer affirmed what the crowd of roughly 3000 spectators already knew. To thunderous applause it was announced that Bannister ran 3:59.4. The unbreakable record had been broken. Roger Bannister had made history.

DEFEATING LIMITING BELIEFS

The 4-minute mile story, however, is not simply about the historic moment of a broken world record. The story of Roger Bannister is about breaking mental barriers and defeating limiting beliefs. At the time, the world of track and field believed the 4-minute mile was an insurmountable human barrier, an impassable obstacle that could not be breached. The critics said it couldn't be done and that it was physically impossible to run a mile under four minutes. It was thought that the heart would stop, the brain would explode, and the lungs would collapse.

As the world scoffed at what it saw as an amateur athlete's unachievable dream, Bannister hardened his resolve to the pursuit of excellence. What makes his feat even more remarkable was that he was dedicated to attain excellence not only on the track, but also in his academic ambitions of becoming a doctor. Bannister believed in himself and he believed in the process to which he had committed himself. As long as steady improvements accrued, he knew the outcome he desired would take care of itself, and that is exactly what happened.

After the myth of the 4-minute mile had been debunked by Bannister, other runners around the world began breaking the 4-minute mile barrier. The week after his historic performance, Bannister and two other runners ran a sub-four-minute mile. Over the course of the following year, thirteen more runners broke the barrier. Within the next two years, exactly 134 runners ran a mile under 4 minutes, and today over 20,000 have been recorded. On July 7, 1999 Hicham El Gurrouj of Berkane, Morocco ran the current world record in 3:43:13. In 1997, Daniel Roman of Kenya ran two miles for the first time ever under 8 minutes in a time of 7:58:61.

This is evidence that there are no physical barriers, only self-limiting barriers. We are the ones who put up these barriers within our own psyche because we choose the beliefs of those around us. You need to unlearn these limitations, and realize that once mental barriers are lifted, anything is possible. The world is perceived differently, and as perspectives change the realm of possibility expands. My goal for you is to have no mental barriers, to believe you are capable of anything you desire. Bannister proved all the naysayers wrong with his positive mentality and self-belief, and now is the time for you to do the same.

SELF-IMAGE OF EXCELLENCE

The field of peak performance has substantiated the notion that as a performer, you will never outperform your self-image. If you believe you are slow, you will perform slowly. If you believe you are fast, you will perform at a fast pace. Therefore, positive thought processes, combined with a solid idea of your goals and how to accomplish them, will give you the best opportunity for your successful accomplishment. In this way, staying positive is symbolic of belief in yourself.

A self-image of excellence is absolutely necessary if you are to embark on the quest to conquer The Mountain of Excellence. You must believe in yourself and your ability to improve throughout the process you have established to achieve your goals. You must believe in your inner excellence and its transcendence to the performances you give on a day-to-day basis. Self-image is a powerful tool in peak performance, which is why it is so important you keep it positive.

INTRODUCTION TO SELF-TALK

When you are playing your best, what are you thinking? When you are at your best what types of words are going through your head? What's that self-talk like?

In peak performance, the little voice talking inside of your head, sometimes becoming outwardly-expressed thoughts directed at yourself, is referred to as self-talk. During performance, this little voice inside your head talks to you constantly. If you are reading this and thinking, "What is this 'voice' Cain is talking about? I do not talk to myself. Only crazy people do that." That would be the voice to which I am referring.

CAIN COACHING POINT:
When referring to self-talk, I often use the analogy of your two mental assassins. You have a green assassin that helps your performance and a red assassin that crushes your performance. You must train your green assassin to win the battle between your ears with positive self-talk.

Everybody has/does self-talk. As an expression of thought, self-talk embodies your mentality towards your performance. We use self-talk to motivate ourselves and to calm ourselves. We use self-talk to encourage ourselves to become fascinated and, unfortunately, self-talk can be used to discourage ourselves when we are frustrated. Self-talk is a reflection of self-image.

When you are performing on the field or in the classroom, the voice in your head is either working for you or against you. Some people visualize the contrasting tones of voice as two little people on your shoulders battling for control over your conscience. Recognize, however, that this self-talk is yours. You own it; you are in control of it.

HARNESS YOUR SELF-TALK

Mastering control of your self-talk can be a challenge. Imagine your self-talk is a mustang, wild and spirited, seemingly uncontrollable. Now, imagine yourself as a Cowboy or Cowgirl who does not wish to strip this wild animal of its fiery spirit, but you do want it to work for you enhancing your pursuit of excellence on the open plains. This is how to think of your self-talk. It is an untamed and powerful beast that has the potential to significantly improve your performance.

To effectively harness your self-talk, you must follow the three steps of performance change. The first step in the process of channeling the power of your self-talk is to establish an awareness of its power over the mind. During performance, try to recognize when you use it and what mentality it reflects – positive or negative. Notice particular situations that bring it out, both the good and the adverse. Notice the particular tones and language used. This is all in an attempt to understand your mental state during, and also away from, performance.

Once you have developed a proficient awareness, the next step in effectively harnessing your self-talk is through a technique called confidence conditioning.

FOCUS ON WHAT YOU WANT VS. WANT TO AVOID –
THE PINK ELEPHANT

Has anyone ever performed the mind tease on you, where they instruct you to focus on something and then say, "Whatever you do for the next 10 seconds, do not think about a pink elephant." Well, naturally the image of a pink elephant pops into your head and you have difficulty focusing on whatever it was you were told to focus on. This little mental tease exemplifies the importance of an individual's ability to keep a focus on what you "want vs. want to avoid" because the brain does not recognize the negative connotation of "do not" and only sees the image of that pink elephant.

The key to ignoring the pink elephants is developing the ability to focus on what you are trying to accomplish, not what you are trying to avoid. If you are a baseball pitcher, think about pounding the strike zone instead of trying not to give up a hit. If you are a hitter, thinking about driving the ball back up the middle instead of trying to not roll over the ball. Academically, when you are taking a test you want to focus on solving the problem or answering the question at hand, not worrying about the next ones. These general scenarios represent the present moment focus that makes the difference between subpar performance and performance excellence.

By channeling your self-talk and focusing on what you want vs. what you want to avoid, you will be competing with a positive mentality that will keep you locked into the present moment giving yourself the best chance for successful results. The ability to focus on what you want with positive self-talk instead of what you want to avoid is a discipline developed over time. This process is dependent on the establishment of routines, such as practicing your self-talk, that assist your focus on proper performance execution in your sport.

CONFIDENCE CONDITIONING

Confidence conditioning is a mental conditioning technique used to harness the power of self-talk to work in your best interest. Confidence conditioning is accomplished by simply writing down a list of statements that give you a sense of strength and empowerment. You can put these confidence conditioning statements on notebook covers, on the wall, on your mirror with a dry-erase marker, on little cards to carry in your wallet, in your locker – really anywhere!

Even though you may not be aware of it, you have been using confidence conditioning statements ever since you could talk. Every time you expressed your belief in the truth of an idea or an experience, you were conditioning it. Mental Imagery, which is simply the creation of vivid mental images, is a natural process, as well. Whenever you imagine something or look forward to it, you were using imagery and conditioning your subconscious. Confidence conditioning and mental imagery are used by a wide variety of people from virtually every walk of life and in every profession. They use these techniques because they are simple to learn, even easier to perform, and they work!

When written and/or put on audio, confidence conditioning is your custom-made blueprint for growth, which provides a consistent frame for your mental imagery and personal development. They are goal statements that help you imagine and realize positive change with minimal stress. If you use them correctly and consistently, they will help you create the athletic career, relationships, and life you most desire.

CONFIDENCE CONDITIONING STATEMENTS

In order to be effective, confidence conditioning statements must be written and used in a way that has the desired impact on your subconscious mind. They must be brief, usually a short sentence, and phrased in the first person, present tense. They must be positive, specific, and realistic. You want to include as many details as possible when writing and they should carry an emotional charge. If they do not make you feel anything, they probably will not help change anything either.

CONFIDENCE CONDITIONING WRITING CHECKLIST

The following are guidelines to help you better write your confidence conditioning statements:

First Person: Confidence conditioning statements are tools that help you to change your self-image; therefore, it makes sense to mentally condition for yourself, because your statements are always about you. They will usually begin with "I."

Present Tense: Use the present tense (I am, I have, etc.) because, in your subconscious, the future and past do not exist. Subconscious time is always "right now."

Positive: Condition and image what you want, not what you do not want or are trying to change. Do not phrase a statement in the negative, such as, "I no longer get anxious when I come to the plate with the game on the line." Instead say, "I remain calm, in-control and focused on what I want to do with this pitch, when the game is on the line." This focuses on what you want to do in the positive.

Indicate Achievement, Not Ability or Potential: In other words, do not say "I can." You already have the potential to change your performance. Instead, create words that describe the end-result you want as if it has already happened by using "I am."

No Comparisons: You are unique and have your own process of development, growth, and change. Do not compare yourself to anyone else or measure your abilities against anyone else's. Just aim for and condition performance change in your own self-image and self-belief.

Vivid & Descriptive Language: In order to "convince" your subconscious that your confidence conditioning statements are real, your language and the images they invoke must be as vivid as possible. Be sure to choose words that help you to really "see" what you are describing.

Emotional Language: Use words that spark an emotional response to make your statements more believable to your subconscious. The more emotion you generate, the faster the change you seek will take place. Describe how you feel about your achievement.

Realistic/Accurate: Do not affirm change that isn't possible or realistic for you. Set your sights neither too high nor too low. Stretch your comfort zone a bit, but do not aim for anything you cannot honestly see yourself achieving. Remember, peak performance is a process. Do not aim for perfection; aim for excellence.

Balance: Make sure that the various goals you condition are in balance with each other. Do not over-emphasize any one area while ignoring others in which growth would be beneficial. Strive for balanced growth and a balanced life.

Confidential: Without intending harm, others may remind you of your old self-image, or they may feel threatened by your desire to change. Keep your statements confidential. You may confide in coaches/mentors, if they understand the confidence conditioning process and are supportive of the changes you are trying to make for the sake of your performance.

TIPS FOR WRITING EFFECTIVE CONFIDENCE CONDITIONING STATEMENTS

1. Change Your Beliefs Before Your Behavior:

It is pointless to condition new behavior when the underlying beliefs driving your old behavior remain unchanged. Write your confidence conditioning statements for both internal beliefs and external behaviors. Failure to change underlying beliefs is one of the main reasons why confidence conditioning will not work for everyone.

BEHAVIOR: I spend an hour of quality one-on-one time with one of my teammates every weekend.

BELIEF: More pressure on an already jammed-up schedule. I'd rather be hanging out with my friends who are not on the team than with my teammates all the time. When do I get my quality time away from my sport?

Do you see the problem? If the underlying belief does not change, it will be impossible to sustain the new behavior. As long as it feels like something you "have to" do, and not something you "want to" do, your creative subconscious will find ways to get you out of it. Try this as an alternative:

BEHAVIOR: I enjoy spending an hour of quality one-on-one time with one of my teammates every weekend.

BELIEF: I look forward to spending time with my teammates every weekend because it is fun, leaves me feeling great about our team, and is building strong relationships that will help us to perform better on the field.

2. Build Personal Value in Your Confidence Conditioning Statements

The positive emotions you feel as you repeat and picture your statements is what makes them "take" in your subconscious. For example:

BELIEF: My health and fitness are major priorities in my life.

BEHAVIOR: I am creative at finding ways to exercise at least one hour a day, six days a week, and I generally eat only nutritious, low-fat foods.

PERSONAL VALUE: Because I exercise and eat right, I feel energized, strong, vibrant, in control, and excellent.

3. Review Your Statements To Imprint Confidence Into Your Subconscious.

Imprinting is simple: READ or LISTEN to your confidence conditioning statements, PICTURE them in your mind, and FEEL the personal value (positive emotions) connected to them. The best times to do this are just after awakening and just before sleep. Review your statements twice a day at a minimum, although more often the better. Make sure you are relaxed (take several deep breaths) and free yourself from distractions. Limit yourself to 10-15 statements to start – you can add more later. Remember, it is the start that stops most people, so take the initiative and get started.

ACTION STEP: CONFIDENCE CONDITIONING WORKSHEET

What do you want to change?

_____

ACTION STEP: CURRENT REALITY

Describe the way it is right now:

_____

Why is it a problem?

_____

How do you feel about the way it is?

_____

Describe your own behavior(s) that you want to change:

_____

What are your deepest beliefs about this situation? Be honest with yourself:

_____

_____

ACTION STEP: VISION (DESIRED NEW REALITY)

Describe the way it will be after the change(s) you seek (use present tense):

Describe the way you will behave to generate the result you want (use present tense):

What beliefs will you need in order to support these new behaviors (use present tense):

How will you feel when you bring your vision into reality? What is the personal value for you?

SAMPLE CONFIDENCE CONDITIONING STATEMENTS

If they accurately express your own goals and feelings, use these examples as written, or use them as models for creating your own powerful confidence conditioning statements.

Remember, you do not have to confine yourself to just personal and professional confidence conditioning statements; imagine growth in any area of life you choose.

SAMPLE PERSONAL STATEMENTS

1. I remain calm and rational when others are upset, frustrated, and emotional, because I have the training to stay in control.

2. I enjoy buying and eating organic, nutritious, water-based, and low-fat foods, because they make me feel healthy and it makes me proud of my dietary choices.

3. I love exercise and work out every day because of the way it makes me feel, look, and for the energy it provides.

4. I am deeply grateful and appreciate all that I have and all that I am, because I am more fortunate than I ever dreamed.

5. I listen attentively when others speak with me and stay in the present moment, because I value relationships.

6. I have great friends that I enjoy spending time with because life is all about relationships and being with people you enjoy and those who enjoy you.

7. I listen attentively when others speak with me. I am a great listener, because communication and relationships are crucial in life.

SAMPLE PROFESSIONAL STATEMENTS

1. It is easy for me to firmly and politely say "no" whenever I feel it is appropriate, because it is not personal, just professional.

2. My career is a great source of satisfaction to me

because it helps me to live, love, learn, laugh and leave a legacy.

3. I bring a natural energy and enthusiasm to work each day because I love what I do and would do it until I die.

4. I am constantly evolving and learning because the journey of excellence has no finish line and the mountain has no summit.

5. I present my ideas persuasively and concisely, in group settings and one-on-one, because communication is the key to unlocking all doors.

6. I make the best use of my time and am always looking for ways to be more efficient and effective, because time is a separator between good and great, and because it is the ONLY factor that is the same among all performers in the world.

7. I am well-organized, systematic, detail-oriented in my work space, because it allows me to be more productive and more efficient.

8. I listen to criticism with an open mind and learn from it or let it roll because I never let ego get in the way of my evolution.

9. I am a source of encouragement and inspiration for my colleagues and they are a source for me, because together we go higher.

10. I speak the truth and get to the point, because being as efficient and effective as possible helps others to grow more quickly.

PERFORMANCE CONFIDENCE CONDITIONING STATEMENTS

During performance, confidence conditioning statements become simplified statements for more memorable self-talk. The requirements for these statements are reduced to reflect the importance that they be present tense, positive, and emotional. All other requirements, however, continue to remain relevant. When you are in your performance arena, use these confidence conditioning statements to maximize your positive mentality.

SAMPLE PERFORMANCE STATEMENTS

1. I command confidence.

2. I trust in my abilities to achieve my goals.

3. Today is mine.

4. I will hit my shots.

5. I have put in the preparation and I am ready to perform.

6. Stay in control, baby.

7. Let the negative go and the positive grow.

8. Focus on the present moment.

9. Dominate the day.

10. Whatever happens, I will be content knowing I gave my best.

Whenever you read one of your confidence conditioning statements, pause for a moment to picture and feel that statement as it if were happening now. Consciously use the self-talk voice within your head to read and recognize the meaning of the statement.

Confidence is essential to the generation of a positive mentality for peak performers. During competition, you must be confident in your ability to perform and trust that all your preparation will pay off. This practice of confidence conditioning not only helps you harness your self-talk voice, but it also builds internal confidence. When the moment of truth arrives in performance, you must believe in yourself and know that when all is said and done, you did your very best. Thus, the process of building confidence will create the positive mentality necessary for your pursuit of excellence.

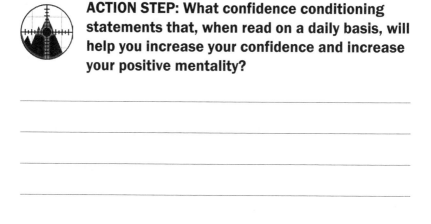 **ACTION STEP: What confidence conditioning statements that, when read on a daily basis, will help you increase your confidence and increase your positive mentality?**

_____

_____

_____

_____

_____

CAIN'S COACHING POINT:
Earlier in this manual we talked about your core values. How are you doing with living out those core values? Are you still setting weekly goals? Your chances for success significantly increase through the simple practice of setting daily goals. Remember, focus on the next 200 feet at a time, working towards improvement, focused on what you want, not what you are trying to avoid.

THE CONFIDENCE RESUMÉ AND LIST OF WINS

Another method of creating positive mentality is to make a confidence resumé and list of wins. The confidence resumé and list of wins is an activity in which you identify all of the wins you have had in your career. Wins in and out of the competitive arena. The purpose of the confidence resumé is to facilitate the development of greater confidence in yourself and your performance by listing all the qualifications that justify why you deserve the outcome you desire.

By nature we as human beings beat ourselves up when we fall short of our goals and briefly celebrate our wins, but always focus on what's next. For example, when you graduated from college, did you really enjoy and take confidence from the body of work you just completed, or were you focused on getting that first job out of school? When you were a child and learned how to ride a bike, did you take confidence from ditching the training wheels, or did you focus on going further and faster? Listing all of yours wins will help you to see the amazing body of work you have done over time and will allow you to have a resource you can review to help build the mental muscle of confidence.

Your confidence resumé and list of wins should include anything and everything that, when reviewed, helps you feel empowered and confident. The confidence resumé and list of wins should be extensive and ongoing. Like climbing The Mountain of Excellence, the confidence resumé and list of wins has no finish line. Your choices can focus on your personal, academic, and athletic skills. They may include previous results, quality preparation, great teammates, books you have read, the people you have met, the places you have been, the wins you have had on the field, the coaches you have played for, doing what was uncomfortable (asking someone out on a date) and celebrating that they said yes, or that you mustered up the courage to ask even though you were turned down. Instead of focusing on the no, focus on the process that you tried.

 Visit www.MentalConditioningManual.com/extras for a sample confidence resumé and list of wins.

 ACTION STEP: Get started with your confidence resumé and list of wins. What are some of the wins you have had in your life that you may have overlooked?

_____

_____

_____

_____

Filling out the confidence resumé is beneficial for athletes because it forces the individual to identify the work they've done and the preparation they've put into the development of the game. This exercise can provide the athlete with either a confidence boost or a look at a sobering reality. Even if the resumé shows you have a lot of work to do, it is important to maintain a positive mentality by realizing you are on the right path and the resumé has given you the constructive criticism you need to succeed.

 **CAIN'S COACHING POINT: In my work with coaches and athletes, even the best athletes on the planet can struggle with developing their confidence resumé. That struggle is exactly why we need to have the confidence resumé in our arsenal as we climb The Mountain of Excellence. Confidence is fragile and every time you review your confidence resumé it will be similar to lifting weights for your confidence and belief. You must do a little a lot to obtain the mental muscles you are looking for. Just as physical muscles take time and effort to develop, so do your mental muscles of confidence.**

After you have written these reasons, post them somewhere you will see them on a daily basis. I have my list on the night stand next to my bed and before I turn the lights out, I review my list and go to bed feeling like a champion. Having this document visible will give you confidence by seeing you have reasons to be. Some teams I work with will create a confidence resumé for the season and review it before each game to remind the team of the hard work and preparation they've done and why they should feel confident during competition. This daily and/or pre-game action is like strength and conditioning for your performance psyche. Through the repetitious acknowledgement of your reasons to be confident, you will steadily build a stronger, more confident mentality. During competition, this should be reason enough to stay positive.

THE SOURCE OF CONFIDENCE

Confidence conditioning will improve positive self-talk and the confidence resumé will augment your belief in yourself and a positive mentality, but both techniques of confidence building rely on a solid base of preparation. True and authentic confidence comes from the combination of actions an individual takes in preparation for performance. Confidence comes from the four key areas:

1) Physical preparation – the BST (Blood, Sweat, and Tears).

2) Positive self-talk & confidence conditioning

3) Performance Routines [Chapter 8]

4) Mental Imagery [Chapter 13]

There is no substitute for smart, hard work. The consistent implementation of effective mental conditioning with your physical conditioning will give you the biggest confidence boost. Physically, you would never do strength and conditioning once a week or once a semester and expect to get any stronger. The same rules apply to mental conditioning, and by integrating it into your physical conditioning, you get the most out of mind and body. Strengthening and conditioning for your mental confidence to enhance confidence is obtained by doing a little a lot, not a lot a little. *You have got to do a little a lot, not a lot a little.* Every time you grind it out in practice and give that extra effort, and every time you take the opportunity to reflect on your confidence conditioning statements and your confidence resumé, you build the mental muscle of confidence.

Conditioning self-confidence is all about building a positive mentality. When it comes down to your performance, all you can do is rely on your preparation and execute in a manner that gives you the best opportunity for the result you desire. You cannot control anything else. You must strive for excellence in practices and competition to give yourself the peace of mind that you have done your best to give your best, and the rest will fall into place.

KEEP YOUR CONFIDENCE HONEST

A great way to keep your confidence honest is through the utilization of an accountability partner(s). There are many different ways for teammates to keep each other accountable for building confidence. Feel free to arrange whatever methods you feel will serve you best. One great way to keep your confidence honest is for your accountability partner to ask you questions about your confidence whenever you see each other. As teammates, if you see each other walking to class or in the dining hall, ask "Tell me two things on your confidence resumé?" "What are three of your confidence conditioning statements?" If you do not respond within a few seconds, then you know you are not reviewing and giving enough focus to your mental conditioning techniques.

During practices, the question I ask players all the time is, "What are you working on today to get better?" If they cannot answer me quickly, they have not properly prepared for practice. They are not present and are not getting the most out of their time at practice that day. They are not building mental confidence and are not building a positive mentality necessary for performance excellence.

FAILURE IS POSITIVE FEEDBACK

In your pursuit of excellence, you will experience failure. This is a fact. Nothing worth having comes easy, and no self-made success story is created without trials and tribulations to overcome. Accept failure as an inevitable part of your journey and learn to view failure as positive feedback.

Failure is actually the most effective form of positive feedback. Failure provides you with the most direct and unequivocal insight into why and how something has gone wrong. If you are trying to accomplish a task, and are giving it your best effort, exercising various techniques but are failing then you are receiving positive feedback from the task on what not to do. This is when you should become fascinated, not frustrated, and realize with each attempt you are exposing the details that will lead you to success.

Remember the prophecy of thoughts, and how your positive or negative thoughts manifest through actions and outcomes. Be positive. Be confident. *Confidence is a choice.* Challenge your limitations and move beyond your mistakes and short-comings by learning from them. The quicker you make mistakes and learn from them, the quicker you move beyond them, and the more prepared you are for the next 200 feet. Choose to be a learner, not a loser, and get better, not bitter. Accept failure as positive feedback.

CAIN'S COACHING POINT: It is important to have the capacity to distinguish when you are getting closer to success and when you are moving further from it. Be sure to ask for advice or counsel when necessary, but be aware that this is your journey. Also, remember that sometimes when the accomplishment you desire feels far away, it actually may be waiting right around the corner.

THE THREE MAGIC LETTERS – YET

When you experience a disappointment in performance and the result you worked so hard to achieve falls beyond your reach, there is a three-letter word to keep your positive mentality – "YET." You can turn statements of failure into goal-setting exclamations by adding this simple three-letter word. This word will turn negative comments around and change your attitude, confidence, and perspective. When you notice you are telling yourself (self-talk) that you cannot do this or that, add the three magic letters "Y-E-T" to the end of your sentence.

I am not in the starting lineup... *YET.*

I cannot hit the ball the other way... *YET.*

I do not throw 90 mph... *YET.*

We didn't win the championship... *YET.*

By adding "YET" to the end of your sentence, you leave the door to your mental hall of excellence open as opposed to slamming the door in your own face. YET is also an acronym for Your Energy Talks, referring to the influence of your energy on yourself, your team, and your goals. When the mood is down and thoughts are negative, use this acronym to remind yourself or others to change the outlook of the situation. Disappointments will occur in your performances, but by treating failures as positive feedback in order to work smarter and harder and by keeping a positive mentality, the results you desire are sure to be on the horizon.

POSITIVE ENERGY IS CONTAGIOUS

Energy is contagious. People subconsciously take cues from others to gauge their own feelings. You probably know when your friends and teammates aren't feeling 100 percent even before they tell you, maybe even before they are aware of it. You definitely know when people are feeling great, because they often exude an aura of positivity that is difficult to ignore. Whether through an outward expression of body language or just feeling a vibe, humans are exceptional at interpreting moods. For better or worse we are so proficient at detecting moods, we often subconsciously take direction from them and mimic that energy in our own actions. The importance of energy in performance should be quite clear.

If energy is contagious, it is obvious you should make that energy positive. Negative energy is simply counterproductive and detracts from gaining momentum for forward progress. A positive attitude when facing the challenges and obstacles of practice or competition goes a long way. Attitude reflects leadership, and if you perform with a positive attitude and bring positive energy on a daily basis, the atmosphere of your team and working environment will begin to reflect your commitment to positive energy. Therefore, if energy is contagious for producing attitudes and attitudes reflect leadership, then leadership, too, is contagious. As you perform, make a concerted effort to build a team of leaders by bringing positive energy to the table.

GET BIG

The term GET BIG refers directly to body language in relation to peak performance. It means to convey a big, confident body language. As you walk down the hall, on the court, on the field, or into your office, your body language is an expression of yourself and conveys a message to those around you.

What happens physiologically and psychologically as you GET BIG is that your brain and body will start to release chemicals that will make you feel more confident. You will start to come up with reasons why you should feel more confident and you will become more confident. Psychology and physiology are a two-way street. You will affect your physical performance by how you think and talk to yourself and you will affect your psychology by how you carry yourself physically; all the while reinforcing a positive self-image.

Again, *I have found that it is easier to act yourself into a way of thinking than it is to think yourself into a form of acting.* You must practice GETTING BIG by consciously walking BIG, and reinforcing confidence by self-talking BIG. GETTING BIG will help you to find the confidence you need to perform at your best. The University of Alabama Softball team, winner of the 2012 NCAA National Championship, understands the importance of GETTING BIG and uses signs of success in their dugout and locker room to remind them of this key peak performance principle.

 ACTION STEP: Where will you hang a GET BIG sign where you can see it each day?

 Visit www.MentalConditioningManual.com/extras for your official Brian Cain Peak Performance GET BIG sign.

SELF-TALK – FINAL THOUGHTS

During performance, your "final thought" symbolizes the last conscious thought in your head before performing a specific action in your sport. The moment before taking the action, you want to narrow your mental focus on a word or phrase that mentally facilitates the physical accomplishment of that action. This final thought should reflect a positive mentality and be confidence-affirming to intensify your focus on the task at hand and thus increase the likelihood of its successful execution.

Too often athletes focus on what they want to avoid, rather than what they accomplish. In baseball, a pitcher whose final thought is, "Do not hit this batter!" represents a completely different mentality from a pitcher whose final thought is "Blow it up!" The same goes for any action in any sport, and the difference in mentality makes a big difference when these thoughts manifest through performance.

Develop your own final thoughts for particular performance actions in your sport. Once you have chosen them, you want to incorporate these final thoughts into your performance routines to augment the mind-body performance connection. Mentally conditioning a final thought will establish confidence by building a routine rhythm to your performance. Developing your own final thought process will undoubtedly help give you the best opportunity for performance excellence.

 ACTION STEP: What are some final thoughts that you could use in your performance?

1) _____

2) _____

3) _____

REALISTIC POSITIVITY

A positive mentality alone will not grant you performance excellence. Do not get carried away with the thought that a positive mentality is the sole element of success, because positivity alone will get you nowhere, you must still take massive action. It is, however, essential to the development of a present moment focus on the process at hand and your overall perception of performance.

Through the adoption and implementation of the positive mentality within all elements of preparation and competitive performance, positivity assists in the execution of performance excellence and gives you the best opportunity to achieve the results you desire. Peak performers, therefore, must be positive performers. Remember, positive mentality alone won't get you anywhere, but its integration within a system of performance excellence is paramount as you climb up The Mountain of Excellence.

CHAPTER #5 REVIEW

- Thoughts manifest through actions and affect outcomes.

- A positive mentality makes a significant difference between educational self-improvement and self-stagnation.

- Defeat limiting beliefs with a positive mentality.

- Keep a positive self-image.

- Self-talk is a reflection of self-image.

- Harness your self-talk through confidence conditioning.

- Your confidence conditioning statements build a positive mentality.

- Confidence resumé facilitates development of confident performance.

- Keep your confidence honest by utilizing an accountability partner.

- Failure is positive feedback; get better, not bitter.

- Turn statements of failure into goal-setting exclamations by adding YET.

- YET - Your Energy Talks.

- Energy is contagious, so make yours positive.

- GET BIG with your body language and self-talk.

- **Use positive final thoughts during performance.**

- **A positive mentality alone won't get you anywhere, but it makes all the difference during your journey.**

NOTES:

NOTES:

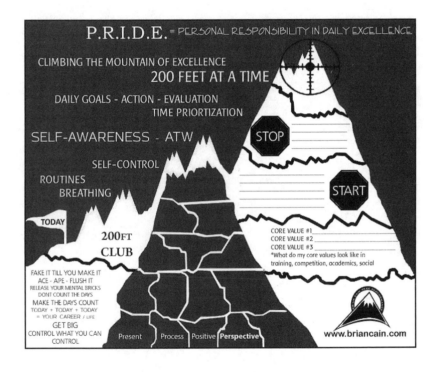

CHAPTER #6

PERSPECTIVE IS REALITY

One of the best movie scenes to illustrate the power of perspective comes from the movie *Dumb and Dumber*, when Lloyd demonstrates the power of perspective in the face of adversity. He has followed Mary, the woman he claims to have been waiting for his entire life, all the way from Boston, Massachusetts to Aspen, Colorado. When the two of them are alone, Lloyd collects himself and musters the courage to ask her an important question. The conversation proceeds as follows:

Lloyd: I like you, Mary. I like you a lot. I want to ask you a question – straight out, flat out, and I want you to give me an honest answer. What do you think the chances are of a guy like you and a girl like me... ending up together?

Mary: Well Lloyd, that is difficult to say. Um, we really do not...

Lloyd: Hit me with it! Just give it to me straight. I came a long way just to see you, Mary. Just... the least you can do is level with me. What are my chances?

Mary: Not good.

Lloyd: You mean not good like 1 out of 100?

Mary: I'd say, more like one out of a million.

Lloyd: So you are telling me there is a chance... YEAH!!!

If you are familiar with the scene, then you are probably chuckling to yourself because you know the full absurdity within this situation. There is, however, value to be found when relating this scene to peak performance.

What is exceptional about Lloyd's perspective is that even though he is presented with a one-out-of-a-million chance, he chose to focus on the fact that Mary responded in a way that even gave him a chance. Although our friend Lloyd's chances of being with his dream gal might not be very good, this scene depicts him choosing to be an optimist, a choice that reflects a championship perspective. Beyond his overt optimism, *he also asks her to clarify and quantify her initial answer to better understand his odds.* Taking this extra step improves the communication process between him and his goal and further develops an awareness of his goal to develop a process to achieve it.

In this chapter, you will learn what a championship perspective is and how to cultivate your own. A constructive perspective is imperative to the development of a peak performer, and will make all the difference not only when performance is going well, but especially when the times get tough. Acquiring a perspective reflective of peak performance will serve you well on your quest up The Mountain of Excellence.

DEVELOP YOUR PERSPECTIVE

A fundamental principle of human psychology and motivation is learning to change your perspective. The most influential coaches of all time have been recorded as having the uncanny ability to discover the excellence and maximize the performance potential within their athletes. These coaches' ability to change the perspectives of their athletes by creating an awareness of performance excellence not previously experienced within themselves is a testament of coaching greatness, but also representative of the potential greatness within us all.

The discovery of this excellence and the maximization of performance potential is what this mental conditioning manual is all about. I want you to find the excellence inside of you, as you transform yourself into a peak performer. I want your team to harness the talents of each individual player for the collective excellence of the team. To discover the peak performer within, you must develop your perspective.

What we see most is often what we notice least. This is called the "law of familiarity" – when you become desensitized to the things around you all the time. This is why, as an athlete, you will often take for granted the fact that you have the technical ability to play your sport, or the fact that you have the education to read this sentence. In your pursuit of excellence, you must learn to see things that you have always seen with a new perspective.

This is critical because it helps you to stay in the present and helps you to appreciate and understand what you have and what you must do to achieve your goals. This leads to an attitude of gratitude and a positive outlook that is necessary when climbing The Mountain of Excellence because you are going to face adversity and failure. You must retain a constructive performance perspective if you are to reach the summit.

FEDERAL EXPRESS LOGO CHANGES LIVES

You have probably heard the saying, *perspective is reality.* This is true in regards to how you interact within the surrounding world, and you can change your life by simply changing your perspective. If you move from a perspective of "I have to" towards a perspective of "I want to." you can dramatically change your emotional and energy state, as well as your performance.

You have probably seen the Federal Express logo below thousands of times in your life. If you change the way you look at the logo, you will change your life. This is the power of perspective.

Take a look between the "E" and the "x." Do you see the white arrow? Was today the first time you have ever seen the white arrow? If so, I can assure you that this arrow has always been there, you just never noticed. Now, from this moment forward and for the rest of your life, whenever you look at the Federal Express logo, you will see that arrow.

What's the point of the arrow? Well, if you have never seen it before, you probably cannot take your eyes off it. You are dumbfounded by the sight of an arrow that you never noticed in a logo with which you are so familiar. Now, ask yourself this question: *"What is inside of you that has always been there and you have never seen before?"*

I want you to start seeing the Federal Express arrow everywhere and in everything. I want you to become encouraged instead of discouraged by adversity. I want you to start to get turned on instead of turned off when things do not go your way. I want you to become fascinated at the prospect of a challenge as opposed to frustrated. Let your haters become your motivators, and let your internal arrow guide your pursuit of excellence.

For the next five days, you will see more Federal Express arrows than you ever have in your life. Every time you see a truck, every time you see a piece of mail, every time you see their advertisement on television or on the internet, you will see that white arrow. That arrow represents your heightened state of awareness, and is the reason you will notice it more. It is not a result of more Federal Express logos in your part of the country over the next five days: it is simply a result of a change in your perspective that has made you more aware.

 ACTION STEP: What is the one perspective you will change to help you climb The Mountain of Excellence?

_____

_____

_____

FAKE IT TILL YOU MAKE IT

This mental conditioning manual is about transforming yourself into a peak performer, so I want you to start to think of yourself as an actor. Not just an athlete, not just a student, not just a friend or family member, but all of those roles and an actor, too. There will be days when you wake up and you do not feel well, but you still have to get the job done. These will be times you are forced to reach within yourself and act differently than how you feel in order to accomplish what is necessary.

This, however, is a constant reality. Whatever you do in life, you will be continuously confronted with situations to which you must respond. This is why it is so important to learn how to take a deep breath, connect yourself with the present moment, and transform yourself into an actor in an attempt to execute a winning performance. As with any other skill, *acting differently than how you feel takes practice,* but you must learn to position yourself in the role that gives yourself the best chance for success.

When you "fake it till you make it," you are changing your perspective by taking control of the game. When you act the way you want to feel, you dramatically increase your chances of finding the energy and emotion you need to perform because, in time, you are going to start to feel the way that you have been acting. *It is easier to act yourself into feeling than it is to feel yourself into action,* and when you fake it, you will not only make it, you will find what you are faking. Ultimately, making the effort to act the way you want to feel will yield a greater performance than allowing yourself to be overtaken by your feelings.

CAIN'S COACHING POINT:

If you are the performer who makes a habit of acting different than how you feel, you might want to do some soul searching. If you fail to prepare and are just constantly acting prepared, time will eventually out you to your audience. "Fake it till you make it" is a technique to be used as an initial motivator for workouts and when necessary in competition, and does not reflect a healthy performance lifestyle. This is a short term technique to help you battle through the grind of climbing The Mountain of Excellence; not a technique that should define your performance mentality.

ACE – ACTING CHANGES EVERYTHING

 The concept of ACE (Acting Changes Everything) builds upon the previous idea that you are an actor, as well as an athlete. You must commit to this belief because acting changes everything. It changes your perception of your situation and the perception others have of you. Remember, perception is reality. Acting is such a powerful art form, the best in the business can produce emotional responses from an otherwise distant audience. An actor's performance can change the audience's perception of reality and produce an intimate connection through viewer empathy and identification with the character played by the actor.

Those who attain their full potential as peak performers are true actors. They have a true passion for their craft and have developed a commitment that transcends the difficult times when they are not feeling like they have their "A"-game.

One of the single greatest examples of how acting changes everything is Game Five of the 1997 NBA Finals, more commonly known as simply The Flu Game. In a series between the Chicago Bulls versus the Utah Jazz, Michael Jordan woke up in Utah before Game Five feeling nauseated and profusely sweating. He was diagnosed with a stomach virus/food poisoning and the Bulls trainers told Jordan there was no way he could play that night. As one of the greatest competitors in the history of sports, Michael Jordan refused to accept a role on the sidelines, especially on the road with the series tied 2-2. What transpired that evening was one of the most memorable games in the history of sports. In one of the greatest individual performances in NBA Finals history, Michael Jordan played 44 minutes of the 48 minute competition and led all scorers with 38 points in the Bullss stunning victory over the Jazz. The Bulls would go on to win the NBA Championship in Game Six.

Jordan's performance is the stuff of legend, but also, it serves as a reminder of the power of mind over matter. Jordan didn't want to rest up to return home for Game Six. He didn't want to stay in bed and dream about the Bulls winning the championship. He didn't want to watch the competition. Jordan wanted to be a part of it and actively contribute the way he believed he could. In Game Five of the 1997 NBA Finals, Michael Jordan acted differently than how he felt in a display of mental excellence that ultimately produced the success he desired. His performance is symbolic of those who are so passionate and committed to their craft that they can act themselves into the role they need to play to succeed, and in the process, make believers out of those around them. What Jordan understood was that acting motivates both oneself and others, while simultaneously changing perceptions of possibility.

Peak performers are those who are always actively acting on their goals, as opposed to passively dreaming about them. They have developed the ability of acting to summon their best when it means the most, despite how they feel. Understanding how to utilize both derivations of the term "acting" is what makes you a peak performer. This is the embodiment of excellence.

Act the way you need to be to succeed, because acting changes everything. This is your ACE in the hole – the ACE up your sleeve.

KNOW YOUR OPPONENT:
PLAY VS. YOURSELF & THE GAME

At the onset of the game, it is important that you understand your opponent. It isn't blue vs. green, or the Beavers vs. the Bears. It is you and your team vs. yourself and the game.

Your greatest opponent will always be yourself. Champions in any arena know that peak performance is contingent on establishing the self-discipline to constantly challenge yourself to improve. At all times, you should be trying to play the game to the best of your ability, whether in practice or in competition. If you execute your skills efficiently and perform at a level higher than the other team, the results of the game will take care of themselves. However, there will always be more competition beyond the championship game, and there will always be new battles to fight and challenges to conquer.

This is why the greatest champions never tire in their pursuit of excellence. They relentlessly push themselves to become the best player they can be, each and every day. The pursuit of the summit on The Mountain of Excellence is a never-ending journey. There is no finish line, for there is always another mountain to climb. That is why you must savor the journey and let go of the destination. Conquering the mountain summit is a daily journey because you cannot live at that altitude. You must be committed to the climb and return to it every single day.

When asked who his greatest competition was over the course of his career, Michael Jordan responded by saying his greatest competitor in basketball was himself. Jordan believed his competitive drive was greater than anyone's, which translated into challenging himself to always improve. For Jordan, this lifestyle goes beyond the basketball court and into the way he lives his life. As an individual, Michael Jordan is the epitome of someone in the pursuit of excellence in all that one does.

PERFECTION IS UNATTAINABLE

Perfection is a concept that is given far too much attention in competitive arenas.

Well, I've got some potentially startling news for you – there is no such thing as perfection!

No matter how hard we try, no matter how hard we want to be, no matter how perfect you believe you are, perfection is unachievable. Perfection is simply a philosophical ideal, not possible in the real world and especially not in sports.

So why does a fictitious concept control so much discussion in athletics? Good question!

Perhaps it is because humans are obsessed by the thought of the unattainable. Perhaps we search for perfection because we are perpetually unsatisfied with our flaws. Perhaps it is a combination of the two.

I believe, however, that the idea of perfection serves as motivation for human improvement. The quest for perfection drives us forward, to work harder and to perform better than in the past. Perfection acts as the ever-present critic that challenges human beings to improve and, through this action, achieve progress.

In this way, perfection represents a double-edged sword. Striving for perfection may be used to motivate people, but never achieving that desired perfection will inevitably dispirit some and act as the constant critic that zaps you of your confidence.

This is why the goal is to pursue excellence over perfection. You will never be perfect. Accept it. Now, move in the direction of going forward with the knowledge that your goal is to be the best that you can be.

At lower levels of competition, perfection is often used to motivate improvement, and this is not a bad practice. However, to focus on perfection at the highest levels of competition will drain your confidence when you encounter adversity and failure. Those who correctly recognize the game as an arena of excellence, not of perfection, give themselves the best opportunity to succeed.

As with all things, there is beauty found in the imperfection of performance. This imperfection gives sport its unpredictability; the reason why we never tire of playing

or watching. As a performer, sport is never as much about perfection as it is progress. Every day, every game, and every season, we aim to be better than we were in our previous performance. This is our true aim as athletes; this is our true aim as human beings.

There never has been and never will be the perfect human being. You will never be perfect, but you can be excellent in your ever-quest for progression. Remember, the goal is to pursue excellence over perfection, and success will take care of itself.

HAVE TO vs. WANT TO

One of the perspective challenges you will be faced with is moving from a "have to" perspective to a "want to" perspective. All competitors are confronted with these two pervasive perspectives, especially in practice and training, and must make the conscious decision to adopt the more positive mentality.

When you tell yourself, "I have to play, I have to work out, I have to compete," you are giving into a negative energy generated by the feeling of some external obligation, which manifests a negative attitude. You do not have to do anything you do not want to. If you truly are discontented with putting in the time to improve something, then maybe you should do some soul searching and do something else.

On the other hand, when you think to yourself, "I want to play, I want to work out, I want to compete," you move your energy and attitude into that constructive mentality. This positive perspective is generated by the feeling of personal preference, when you feel in control of yourself and enjoy what you are doing.

As a peak performer, you must turn your "have to's" into "want to's" whenever you recognize yourself feeling obligated to perform. For example, you do not get out of bed at 6:00 am to go work out because it is the only time you can fit in. You get up and work out because you want to, for reasons x, y, and z. Converting to a "want to" perspective will help you get any job done.

COMPARED TO WHAT?

During the course of cultivating a championship perspective, three of the most powerful words to be conscious of are: "Compared to what?" This three-word question has enormous significance for transforming daunting undertakings into reasonable tasks. Peak performers know how to utilize this question to shift their perspective on the work at hand. They learn that, when faced with the prospect of a challenge, they take a moment to reflect and ask themselves, "Compared to what?"

Peak performers realize that the world is full of people who are less fortunate than others. The importance of perspective is premised on the fact that no matter how difficult a situation you are in, someone out there is in a more difficult one. If you are a college student and you do not want to go to class or do the reading because it is laborious, ask yourself, "Compared to what?" Compared to manual labor performed by the person who never had an opportunity to receive a college education? If you are an athlete and you wake up for an early morning team practice and you are feel tired, ask yourself. "Compared to what?" Compared to the exhaustion felt by the soldier stationed in a hostile area who has to wake up for an early morning lookout shift, knowing his comrades' lives are in his hands? I hope you get the picture.

You see, adversity is inevitable. Everyone deals with it one way or another. But, the people who are most effective in dealing with adversity do so by maintaining a positive perspective. When faced with adversity, they use the three magic words to regain their positive perspective: "Compared to what?" This phrase places all adverse tasks into a realm of possibility.

Perspective is about appreciating what you have and the opportunities before you. We are all privileged in our own unique ways, so focusing on what makes a task difficult is a waste of time. Instead, you have the ability to focus on what makes the task easier for yourself. My mother always told me that if 10 people stood in a circle and all threw their issues into the center, you would be happy to take yours back. Someone, somewhere always has more challenges to overcome than you do. So, stop making excuses and change your perspective by developing an attitude of gratitude. Identify a constructive process you can follow to help bolster your psyche as you continue on your journey up The Mountain of Excellence.

PERSPECTIVE POSTER

A highly effective way to cultivate a constructive perspective is to create your own personal perspective poster. The poster should be a collage of visual representations that remind you of the adversity that other people face on a daily basis. This poster may consist of pictures of inspirational people who overcame adversity to achieve great accomplishments, quotes that elicit motivation and perseverance, and symbols that reflect stories of greatness from humble and adverse beginnings.

When I recognize myself using negative self-talk, carrying mental bricks, or facing a difficult situation, I will often look to my perspective poster to help me regroup and regain perspective. It reminds me that there are many people who have it way worse than I do, and they have overcome their adverse situations. This thought process reminds me of how I am privileged and that I must stop making excuses and focus on forward progress, one step at a time.

The process of creating this poster will benefit your sense of perspective by forcing you to thoughtfully reflect upon the privileges within your life and adversity in all its forms. It will also make you consider what people and stories inspire you and who you admire for overcoming great adversity. The perspective poster can also be a great team-building activity, where each athlete shares his personal perspective poster with the team and then selects one image to include in the team's perspective poster.

When you have completed your poster, I recommend that you hang it someplace visible; e.g. on your wall, the back of your door, or in your locker, to maintain the "Compared to what?" mentality. If you have a team perspective poster, it can be hung in the locker room or a dugout. When you surround yourself with visual representations of those who face and overcome great adversity, it becomes easier to maintain a positive and hopeful perspective. It serves as a constant reminder of your privilege, while motivating you to seize the opportunity to perform the tasks at hand.

There is no right way or wrong way to create your poster, as long as when you look at it, your poster reminds you of the "Compared to what?" mentality. On my perspective poster I have images of lost loved ones, clippings from 9/11, photos of people who have overcome tremendous odds to be successful, and people who have lived their lives the right way and are a source of inspiration to me.

My personal perspective poster hangs in my office and travels with me in my mental conditioning manual in my day planner and on my iPhone as a photo.

 Visit www.MentalConditioningManual.com/extras to see an example of Brian's personal perspective poster and a team poster.

PERSONALIZING PERFORMANCE

For many competitors, keeping their sport and performance in perspective is difficult. Athletes often allow their sport to consume their lives, which leads to the issue of personalizing performance. Personalizing performance is the result of seeing one's self-worth only as the product of his performance in the competitive arena of his sport. This is not healthy for maintaining a positive mentality.

It is imperative that you keep your sport and performance within a big-picture perspective. I have worked with many athletes who hold the wrong perspective. They think the outcome of their performance is reflective of their self-worth. Many athletes will say, "I have got to eat, breathe, and sleep my sport," which is often what it takes to compete at the highest level. *This mentality, however, becomes problematic when they internalize their roles as athletes to the point where success in their sport is the only measure of their life's meaning and as the only way for them to be successful. This perspective is as problematic as it is untrue.*

It is easy, however, to see why an athlete's self-worth can get wrapped up in the sport they play. Because sport plays a large role in their life and people identify them as athletes, their identity naturally tends to become that of an athlete. If you are a college athlete, for example, anytime you get a phone call or an email from someone you went to high school with or from a parent, one of the first questions asked is about your sport. "How's [insert your sport] going?" "How're you playing?" "How's the team this season?" Most student athletes report that they get asked these questions before being asked about academics or their social life. This further engrains the idea of "athlete" as the dominant identity, which only further drives these students towards personalizing performance.

Many athletes I work with fall into the trap of believing their performance in their sport is more than a reflection of their self-worth as a person. If they perform well, they are happy and a positive person to be around. If they do not perform well, they are miserable and just want people to stay away from them. This is not healthy and is not conducive to peak performance. Remember, consistency wins. Those who are able to maintain a positive perspective on a consistent basis give themselves the best opportunity to achieve excellence.

SPORT IS WHAT YOU DO, NOT WHO YOU ARE

If you can relate to this, check your perspective, because you might be personalizing performance.

One of the most important ways to maintain a healthy mentality and a positive perspective is to understand that sport is what you do, it is not who you are. This simple message is pertinent to not only student and amateur athletes, but also professional athletes and coaches, as well. In recognizing that your sport is something you do and accepting that it does not define you as a person, you relieve yourself of a sizable amount of self-imposed pressure.

It is not difficult to recognize the increased pressure the athlete places onto his/her shoulders as a result of personalizing performance. This is why one of the big perspective changes an athlete must make is to see himself as a person who participates in sport, not as an athlete who then participates in life. As mentioned in the previous section, this can be difficult to accomplish when most people define an athlete solely by his role in athletics. As an athlete, you must resist this, reclaim your identity, and identify yourself as an individual who does athletics.

 ACTION STEP: Who are you outside of your sport? What other characteristics do you possess that make you more than just an athlete?

1) _____

2) _____

3) _____

4) _____

5) _____

This transformation in perspective can be difficult for many athletes, because they've allowed their sport to define their identity. If you can relate to personalizing perspective, take a moment to reflect on all the things you do outside of athletics, because at some point your sporting career will come to an end. This is a universal and inevitable part of being an athlete, because you cannot play for your entire life. So, what are you going to do when your career is over? Think about it.

 ACTION STEP: We can't play our sport forever. What will you do when you career is over? Start developing a list now and start exploring some of those ideas in order to give yourself the best chance for life success after your career as an athlete is over.

1) _____

2) _____

3) _____

Many athletes refuse to think about life beyond their sporting career. They believe this long-term perspective will compromise their dedication to their sport, ultimately compromising their ability to succeed. This belief must change. While peak performance is contingent on present moment focus, it is also imperative that you balance this practice with a big picture-perspective. Appreciating that sport is what you do, not who you are allows you to immerse yourself in the present moment and perform to the best of your abilities. It begets a deeper understanding of who you are outside of the sports arena, enabling a clarity of perspective that gives you the best opportunity for performance excellence.

SEGMENTATION & SEPARATION

Once you are aware of the significant difference between the person you are "in sport" and the person you are "out of sport." the next step is to actively facilitate the transformation. In mental conditioning, the process that facilitates the separation of your performing-self and your real-self is known as segmentation. Segmentation is best described as the establishment of pre-game and post-game routines that serve to transform a person from their real-self into their performing-self for their performance and conversely, when the competition is over, out of their performing-self and back into their real-self.

If you didn't know before – SURPRISE! – you have two selves. Your real-self represents who you are outside of competition, while your performing-self represents who you need to be when the uniform is on. Who you choose to be when you are your real-self (with your family, at class, in social settings) is your decision. Who you need to be when you are your performing-self should be identified by you and your coaches. Most professionals have the ability to segment their personal lives and their professional lives, as they have grown to understand and distinguish between the two. The establishment of segmentation routines is the most effective method to facilitate the mental processes of the athlete's self-transformation, and in Chapter 8 you will learn some specific techniques to supplement this transformation.

YOU CAN BE TWO COMPLETELY DIFFERENT PEOPLE

Do you need to be more aggressive during performance? Do you need to be more confident? Have a higher volume when you communicate? If so, eliminate the excuse of, "That is just not who I am." Start to focus on changing your perspective of who you are and becoming who you need to be to succeed. Your performing-self and your real-self CAN be two completely different people. This is the purpose of segmentation; your pre-performance routine will help you to get into the competitor mindset and your post-performance routine will help you to get back into your real-self mindset.

Here I will share stories of two athletes I have worked with who do this beautifully: Chad Cordero and Georges St. Pierre.

CHAD "THE CHIEF" CORDERO

Chad Cordero is a former Major League Baseball relief pitcher who broke into the big leagues with the Montreal Expos less than two months after they drafted him as the 20th overall pick in the first round of the 2003 MLB Draft. From 2005-2007 he racked up 113 saves, the second most in the National League behind Trevor Hoffman's 131.

In June 2005, Cordero tied the major league record for saves in one month with 15 and was on the 2005 National League All-Star team. On June 13, 2007, Cordero (at age 25 years and 86 days) became the second youngest player in baseball history to reach 100 saves in a career.

Chad was a great teammate at Cal State Fullerton from 2001-2003 when I was there as a graduate assistant coach. He is one of the nicest, easiest-going human beings you will ever meet. However when he stepped on that pitcher's mound, be it a game or in practice, he was a different dude.

His presence was one of intense focus and domination. He looked like he would kill you if that was what he had to do to win. He really knew how to shift gears and perform excellently, regardless of how he felt physically.

This type of self-transformation is illustrative of a peak performance perspective shift. While performing in practice or competition, you should strive to lock into your peak performance perspective of mental toughness, and then be able to walk away from that perspective when your performance is over. Chad has always been a prime example to me as someone who understood the difference between his real-self and his performing-self, and had a great career by understanding peak performance perspective.

GEORGES "RUSH" ST. PIERRE

Ultimate Fighting Championship superstar Georges St. Pierre is much like Cordero in that, outside of the Octagon, he is one of the nicest, most humble, and down-to-earth men you will ever meet. Once he turns off his phone and gets out of his street clothes or suit, as a part of his pre-training or pre-fight segmentation routine, and into his fight gear, so too, goes that nice guy mentality (real-self) and out comes the mixed martial arts warrior (performing-self).

Balancing these perspectives shows maturity and intelligence, both of which Georges has plenty. Georges is a world-class person and a world-class fighter. He is able to maintain both personas because he knows who he is and, just as importantly, who he needs to be, and when he needs to be it.

ACTION STEP: Explore your performing-self. Who do you need to become, what competitive character traits do you need to develop to give yourself the best chance for success?

1) _____

2) _____

3) _____

CRABS IN A BUCKET

 Have you ever been to the beach and tried to catch crabs and put them in a bucket? If you only catch one crab, you had better put a cover on the bucket, because that lone crab will likely escape. If you catch multiple crabs, however, no cover is necessary. The crabs actually keep each other in the bucket. When one tries to climb to freedom the others grab at his legs and pull him down, ensuring the collective demise of all.

This "crab mentality" is evident when the group or team will attempt to "pull down" a member who achieves success beyond his peers out of envious emotions and competitive feelings. Or, "If I cannot have it, neither can you." This crab mentality is not something desired in team sports, or life in general, and has no place in peak performance as you climb on your journey to the summit of The Mountain of Excellence.

In athletics, the term "crab" describes an individual with short-sighted, non-constructive thinking rather than a unified, long-term, constructive perspective. As we continue to work through this manual, you may notice that some teammates think they are too cool for the mental game and become overtly negative about learning new material. Unfortunately, these crabs are everywhere in life, and you need to be consciously aware that those who are unwilling to help themselves are not worth your time, if you are in pursuit of performance excellence. Stick to what you do and do not let their negative perspectives pull you down.

Right now, I want you to reflect on some of the crabs in your life. Who are some of the people who pull you down and tell you that you cannot accomplish your goals? Who are the people who tell you that you are never going to make it? Who are the people you hang out with that hold you back? Brainstorm your list below.

 ACTION STEP: The people who I would consider crabs, because they tend to pull me down more than lift me up, are:

_____

_____

_____

_____

_____

If you do notice a teammate adopting a crab mentality, express concern to that teammate, your coaches or your team captain to help this individual get back on the right path to being a team player. It is important for individuals to have a collective mentality in order to create a unified atmosphere for the entire team to metaphorically get out of the bucket – a feat of unified performance excellence.

CAIN'S COACHING POINT:
It is said that you will become the average of the five people with whom you spend the most time. Choose your close company carefully and wisely.

WAR DOGS

Since ancient times, dogs have been trained as a valuable weapon for times of war. A war dog is a dog trained specifically for the battlefield. Their jobs have varied over the years, from attacking with the infantry and mauling the enemy in battle, to sensing trouble nearby with their sharp sense of hearing, or to sniffing out mines in the battlefield with their acute sense of smell. Sometimes these war dogs will even step on a mine or get in the way of enemy fire to save a soldier, sacrificing their lives for the betterment of the team.

When I work with a team, I use the term "War Dog" for those select few who give everything to the team – those who always place the team first and foremost. For an athlete to be called a War Dog is the highest of honors, bestowed only to those who are the greatest teammates and who have truly earned it, both in and out of the performance arena.

If you are reading this and think that you may not make the team, that you may be getting cut, do you have what it takes to put your ego aside? To be selfless? To be a War Dog? Can you choose the perspective of putting the team ahead of yourself and doing anything you can to help the team? That is truly the perspective of champions.

If you have the right type of attitude, the right type of work ethic, but do not have the physical skill yet to play the game at that level, you can still be a great teammate. You can still be the War Dog on your team. War Dogs have the constructive perspective necessary to motivate the team and lead by example to achieve collective performance excellence.

What are you going to do to help your teammates? Can you be the War Dog who throws batting practice all day so your coach can go instruct? Will you be that War Dog who can hit ground balls or do anything that is asked with a smile on your face. If you strive to be a War Dog, peak performance will ultimately be achieved and your inner excellence will shine through.

A WAR DOG REWARDED

Jonah Bayliss was a high school baseball teammate of mine and when I was a senior, he was a junior. He was the number three or four pitcher on our team which meant that he did not play very much. What he did do, was embrace the role of war dog and prided himself on being the most excellent teammate and foul ball shagger you have ever seen. If there was a foul ball, Bayliss was sprinting after it and demanded that someone time him so that he could break a record. Measurement is motivation.

His perspective on being the best he could be at everything he was doing and putting the team above himself was truly selfless and truly reflected a champion's perspective. The amazing part of the story is that he went on to play Division III college baseball at Trinity College in Hartford, Connecticut, and became a seventh round draft pick in the 2002 MLB Draft, culminating in a successful career at the Major League level.

He was able to apply the perspective he had developed as a devoted teammate at Mt. Greylock Regional High School as a role player and war dog eventually playing in Major League Baseball. This epitomizes the fact that a peak performance perspective is essential to reaching the summit of The Mountain of Excellence. Jonah is a living example of a War Dog rewarded by the game.

GET THE REAL INFORMATION

One of the most important parts of creating a peak performance perspective is getting the real information. When you have a discussion with your accountability partners, do you want them to tell you what you want to hear or do you want the honest truth that may be difficult to hear? Whether it is a friend, teammate, coach, or family member you rely on for support to achieve your goals, you must understand that honesty and constructive criticism are the best feedback these people can provide to you. The real information makes all the difference in building a strong perspective. Feedback is the breakfast of champions.

ACTION STEP: Who are the people you go to when you want an honest answer? Who are the few people in your life who will give it to you straight?

1) _____

2) _____

3) _____

CHANGE YOUR PERSPECTIVE

Work to adopt and develop a peak performance perspective by believing that giving your best every day will ultimately result in the achievement of excellence. Work to compete against yourself and accept challenges with a "Compared to What?" perspective. I want you to develop the ability to segment and separate between your performing-self and your real-self. I want you to see more Federal Express arrows in the world around you while realizing that this world is not perfect, and neither is your performance – but it can be excellent. The development of this kind of constructive perspective is necessary to achieve peak performance and it will make the view from the summit of The Mountain of Excellence all the more excellent.

CHAPTER #6 REVIEW

- Develop a perspective that defeats the "law of familiarity."

- See the Federal Express arrow (what has always been there that you have never seen before) everywhere and in everything, especially inside of you.

- Fake it till you make it.

- ACE – Acting Changes Everything.

- You are your greatest opponent.

- Compete against yourself and the game.

- There is no such thing as perfection.

- Pursue excellence over perfection and success will take care of itself.

- Move from a "Have To" perspective to a "Want To" perspective.

- When faced with a difficult or laborious task, ask yourself, "Compared to what?" for motivation.

- Adversity is inevitable, embrace it.

- Perspective posters help you develop an attitude of gratitude and the "Compared to what?" mentality.

- Keep your sport in perspective; do not personalize performance.

- Sport is what you do, it is not who you are.

- Know how to separate between your performance-self and your real-self.

- Adjust your perspective to access all your performance potential.

- Do not let the "crabs" in your bucket pull you down.

- Become a War Dog.

 www.MentalConditioningManual.com/extras
For BONUS Mental Conditioning Material &
FREE Peak Performance Training Tools

NOTES:

NOTES:

NOTES:

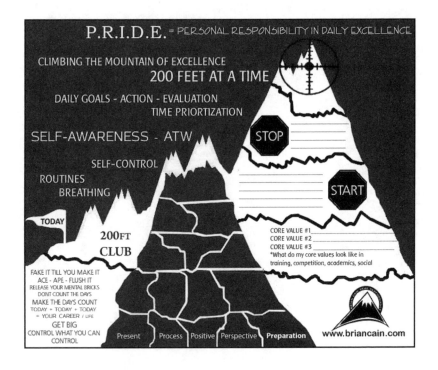

CHAPTER #7

CHAMPIONSHIP PREPARATION

In 2004, the California State University, Fullerton baseball team completed the first half of their season with a 15-16 record. At this midway point in the season, the team made the collective promise to turn their season around by placing their collective faith and trust in their preparation. In one of the greatest single season turnarounds in college baseball history, Cal State Fullerton would go on to win the NCAA Division I National Championship with a final record of 47-22.

The Titans and their head coach George Horton were able to turn their season around with a commitment to the fundamentals and an intense focus on preparation, both physical and mental. I was a member of the Fullerton staff in 2002 and 2003, and know firsthand that Coach Horton is a firm proponent of competing every day in practice as if it were a national championship game. I've seen firsthand how to replicate championship intensity in practice with proper structure and commitment to the preparation process.

When the team reached the College World Series in Omaha, Coach Horton brought a water bottle filled with dirt from the team's field in Fullerton. Before the start of the College World Series the team went out on to the field and sprinkled that Fullerton dirt on the mound and in the batter's box of Rosenblatt Stadium, Official Home of the NCAA College World Series. This action served as a reminder to his players of all the hard work and preparation put in every day of practice back home, and that performance on the biggest stage of college baseball was no different than back home.

The game remains the same anywhere you play; nothing changes. It reminded players that the goal was to do the same thing in Omaha that they did every day in Fullerton – to continue to play against themselves and the game, throw quality pitches, have quality at-bats and play quality defense. It reminded the team that they compete as hard as anyone in the country on a daily basis in practice and that is what they were going to do in Omaha – nothing changes. It was clear that Horton and the Titans trusted their preparation, because the result took care of itself.

CHAMPIONSHIP PREPARATION

Legendary UCLA basketball coach John Wooden wrote in *A Lifetime of Observations and Reflections On and Off the Court* that his practices were so hard, so fast-paced, and so competitive that when UCLA played against other universities, his players would often remark that it felt like the games were in slow motion. It seemed this way because the tempo of these games was, in fact, slower than practices. When the teams stepped out onto the basketball court, Coach Wooden's practice philosophy gave his team a psychological edge over the competition. As Coach Wooden's ten NCAA national championships confirm, his practice philosophy was the epitome of championship preparation.

MENTAL PREPARATION

Mental preparation is fundamental to peak performance. In the words of John Wooden, "Nothing is better preparation for intense game pressure than countless hours of disciplined effort spent mastering the fundamentals." In this chapter, we focus on mastering the fundamentals of mental preparation through the implementation of effective mental conditioning practices and techniques.

Performance reflects preparation, and these strategies aim to cultivate a peak performance mentality as you practice for your performances, as well as the practices of your daily life. This chapter will help you establish a disciplined effort in developing a lifestyle of performance preparation.

GAME-LIKE PRACTICE

Game-like practice is essential for enhanced mental preparation. If you want to perform at a level of excellence, you must practice at a level of excellence. Practice is performance. The dictionary definition of "practice" is "to perform (an activity) or exercise (a skill) repeatedly or regularly in order to improve or maintain one's proficiency." This definition illustrates what peak performers must internalize: repetition of quality performance is fundamental to the achievement of excellence.

Coaches are always telling players that you will play like you practice, so you should practice like you play. This is contingent, however, on making practices game-like. The purpose of game-like simulations is to help familiarize athletes with the conditions they will face in the heat of competition. Repeated exposure to game-like conditions is the best method to mentally condition for the real thing. When your time comes to perform on the big stage, if you already put in the hard work to accustom yourself to the environment, it will pay off through your performance.

As the celebrated 20th century American author Ray Bradbury said, "I know you have heard it a thousand times before. But it is true – hard work pays off. If you want to be good, you have to practice, practice, practice. If you do not love something, then do not do it." This sentiment is dead on. If you have the love and desire to be excellent at what you do, then practice, practice, practice.

It is worth emphasizing that practice must be of proper quality to render desired results. Repetition of a poor quality performance will result in just that; whereas excellent quality will produce performance excellence. Remember, repetition alone does not bring rewards but the quality matters.

REWARDED BEHAVIOR = REPEATED BEHAVIOR

The inverse of the notion that quality repetition brings rewards is also true. As extensive research in developmental psychology espouses, rewarded behavior becomes repeated behavior – true for both poor and quality behavior. By rewarding specific steps in the preparation process when executed properly, the development of skill proficiency is enhanced. Coupled with simulated competition, game-like practices, athletes place themselves in the best environment to cultivate performance excellence.

What an athlete wants to hear most is his name attached to a specific positive compliment. As you pass out praise to your teammate, the more specific you can be, the more beneficial the impact of that praise. Telling Brian that he did a good job means very little because Brian does not hear exactly what he did to receive the positive complement. Telling Brian that he did a great job hustling down the first baseline after getting jammed with an inside fastball and putting pressure on the defense which almost caused them to make an errant throw, rewards him for his effort running to first base. This will yield more of the same effort in the future. Through this positive reinforcement, rewarding proficiency will ultimately improve performance.

STRATEGIES FOR GAME-LIKE PRACTICE

1. Make it competitive – have a winner and loser for everything. If there is a winner and loser when you play in competition, structure that same competitiveness within your daily practices so that everything you do simulates that competitive intensity. Athletes love competition, so giving athletes more opportunities to compete will increase intensity and enhance development. Giving each player an individual win and loss record for competitions held each day and then posting these win and loss records so that they can be seen each day, helps to show who the best competitors and best winners are in your program. Competing against each other sets standards of excellence in practice that will help take your practice competitiveness to the next level.

2. Different colored practice uniforms will help to create a separation between the two teams and give the practice a more competitive flavor. Every college program I work with has practice uniforms. Very few of the high school programs I work with do. When you put the practice uniform on, it becomes part of your routine and helps an athlete's segmentation. Athletes also appear more uniform when in uniform, which seems only appropriate. This emphasizes the importance of the team as a unit, setting the stage for the collective "we" over the individual "me".

If you can break out your game uniforms, this is a great opportunity for each player to see if their uniform fits comfortably and does not hinder any physical movements. It also helps create that competitive environment of two teams going head-to-head to enhance competition.

3. Bring in officials when you scrimmage. This will free up

coaches and athletes on your team from having to make the calls. It will also increase the competitive nature of the scrimmage because it is more game-like.

4. Use a scoreboard so that the coaches and athletes can keep track of the stats just as you would in competition. Creating a process-based scoring system in which you give points for specific aspects of performance is also a great way to reward the behavior you want in your team. For example, giving three points to the team whose player takes a charge and draws an offensive foul in a basketball scrimmage will reward the type of behavior desired in games. It will also give instant feedback to the team that a charge is worth as much as hitting a three-point shot.

PROCESS-BASED SCORING SYSTEM

A strategy to make practice more game-like is to create a process-based scoring system for intra-squad scrimmages. Under the premise that rewarded behavior becomes repeated behavior, points are earned for a player's effort and execution of particular skills rather than just points, runs, goals, or whatever standard scoring measurement is used in your sport.

Coaches often choose to use process-based scoring systems during practice to highlight particular skills in which the team must improve. I often recommend coaches begin using this system to focus on one particular skill at a time. As players familiarize themselves with the framework of the system that the coach has implemented, the coach may introduce and highlight more skills to monitor. This process-based scoring system is, like all systems of preparation, one of steady progression. Coaches may even add different dimensions to the scoring system, such as taking away points or giving points to the other team for anything seen as disrespect in the game.

Below is an example of a process-based scoring system for football.

DEFENSIVE

TOUCHDOWN – 6 pts

TURNOVER – 4 points

3 & OUT – 3 points

DRIVE STOP – 2 points

SACK – 2 points

TACKLE FOR LOSS – 2 points

FORCE FUMBLE – 1 point

SPECIAL TEAMS

BLOCKED FG – 3 points

BLOCKED XPT – 1 point

OFFENSIVE

TOUCHDOWN – 6 points

FIELD GOAL – 3 points

15-YD RUN PLAY – 3 points

20-YD PASS PLAY – 3 points

2-PT CONVERSION – 2 points

FIRST DOWN – 1 point

EXTRA POINT – 1 point

Visit www.MentalConditioningManual.com/extras for more process-based scrimmage scoring sheets.

CAIN'S COACHING POINT:
The process-based scoring system can be changed to fit your program needs and you can award points for any part of the process that you wish to emphasize.

Below is an example of a process-based scoring system for basketball.

PROCESS-BASED SCRIMMAGE SCORING SYSTEM		VISITOR	HOME
PACE OF THE GAME			
Sprint off the court (time out, quarters, half)	+1		
DEFENSE			
Pass deflection	+1		
Steal	+2		
Defensive rebound	+2		
5-second call – 10-second call	+2		
Diving on floor	+3		
Aggressive ball pressure – dead dribble	+1		
Excellent verbal communication	+1		
Help defense	+2		
Take a charge	+4		
Aggressive contact on a defensive block out	+2		
Close out	+2		
Defensive awareness to win	+2		
OFFENSE			
Assist	+1		
Pass to the post	+1		
Setting a screen that gets a teammate a shot	+2		
Setting a screen	+1		
Diving on the floor for a loose ball	+3		
Offensive rebound	+3		
Going hard to the offensive boards	+1		

Process-based scoring system for baseball and softball.

PROCESS BASED SCRIMMAGE SCORING SYSTEM		VISITOR	HOME
PACE OF THE GAME			
Team energy and dugout intent and participation	+1		
Off the field in 10 sec (OF) and or 5 sec (INF)	+2		
Around INF after strikeout (6) or out at first (5)	+2		
PITCHERS			
Win the 1-1 count (only awarded to p)	+1		
First pitch thrown for a strike (only awarded to p)	+1		
No freebies = HBP, BB, PB, WP, SB, error	+4		
1-2-3 inning	+2		
12 pitches or less in an inning	+2		
Winner of 3-2 battle	+2		
DEFENSE			
Web gem	+2		
Double play	+4		
2.0 by catcher between innings on throw to 2Bw/tag	+2		
Throw out lead runner with tag	+4		
OFFENSE			
Any freebies = HBP, BB, PB, WP, SB, error	+2		
Bunt base hit	+2		
Aggressive base running	+2		
Situational hitting	+2		
Leadoff or a 2 out BB/HBP	+2		
8 pitch at bat	+2		
2 out RBI	+4		

RUNS IN AN INNING	1	2	3	4	5	6	TOTAL
VISITOR							
HOME							
SITUATIONAL EX (E)	1	2	3	4	5	6	TOTAL
VISITOR							
HOME							
PROCESS PTS (H)	1	2	3	4	5	6	TOTAL
VISITOR							
HOME							

Runs Column = Runs Scored
Hits Column = Process Points
Errors = Situational Scrimmage
MUST USE Scoreboard, Umpires,
Two Color Shirts

MOVE THE RUNNER SCRIMMAGE
1 Point Both Teams: Advance Runner & Hitter Out
2 Points Offense: Both Runners Safe
2 Points Defense: Get Lead Runner Out

1st & 2nd = Runner at 1st – Sac Bunt Move Runner – 3rd & 4th = Runner at 2B – Hit & Run 5th & 6th = Runner at 3B, 1-Out – Score Runner

In situational scrimmage, pitcher is throwing a fastball for a strike down the middle.

I've seen these process-based scoring systems implemented to encourage performance excellence in everything a team does during preparation. If there is a non-hustle play, two points go on the board for the other team. If there is team energy and involvement, players getting excited for a sacrifice bunt, they get two runs on the scoreboard. After the third out is made, if the infield gets across the foul line in six seconds and the outfield gets across in twelve, points are awarded because getting on and off the field is significant in doing little things excellently. It is the little things like getting on and off the field that look good but, more importantly, it adds pace and tempo to the game and gives you a competitive advantage.

EXTRA EFFORTS OF EXCELLENCE

To further emphasize the significance of excellent preparation in all things, no matter how small, let's explore the importance of extra efforts. By elaborating on the importance of the aforementioned example of returning to the dugout in a timely manner, the crossover effect from preparation to competitive performance becomes clear. For example, if you are facing a talented pitcher and your defense gets off the field, then your team can get in the dugout, get its bats, batting gloves and helmets, and get out in front of the dugout with enough time to go through your batting routine and warm-up pitches. The extra effort to make a prompt return to the dugout gives you more time to prepare for a quality at-bat, and should become a routine element of your in-practice performance that transfers to game time.

This example of extra effort applies on the other end of the rotation as well. If you are the third out of the inning offensively and you sprint back on the field to play defense with the rest of your team while your pitcher throws his warm-up pitches, it is going to tip control of the tempo in your favor. The next thing the other team realizes is, the umpire's yelling, "hitter, hitter, let's go" because they took their time getting off the field. Now, you immediately have the competitive advantage. This puts the leadoff hitter into red lights because your team has sped up the game on the opposition. By making the extra effort to apply pressure to the leadoff batter you increase the likelihood of getting the out. It is been statistically measured that when the leadoff hitter gets on base, his team improves its chances of scoring in that inning to 54% as opposed to the 14% percent chance of scoring within the inning if the leadoff hitter gets out.

This illustrates the true value of extra efforts of excellence in creating a competitive advantage. If baseball is not your sport, think about the extra effort you can give in particular areas of your sport, and brainstorm how to make statistics play in your favor.

PRACTICE MAKES PERMANENT

Practice does not make perfect, but practice makes permanent. It is the quality of your practice that gives you the best chance for quality performance. If your practice is high or low quality, you can be certain your performance will reflect it. Also, notice that I am highlighting quality instead of quantity. I mentioned the value of quality repetition earlier, and it cannot be overemphasized. You can practice something all day long, but if you have practiced the wrong technique, all that preparation means little. It is not the quantity, but the quality that counts. This is also why proper mental conditioning is so significant, because if you do not exercise a winning mentality, you are bound to lose.

It is your obligation in your pursuit of excellence to utilize your preparation time to make the right skills permanent. As athletes, we do not often, if ever, have control over the situations in competition. In practice, however, the control is ours. In practice, you control the repetition of rehearsing plays and running-through game-like scenarios. In practice, you can try something over and over again. Take advantage of that time, because we all know that when game time rolls around and the stakes are elevated, you only have one shot to get it right. This is also why elevating the level of practice to simulate game-like intensity is beneficial. Recognize that practice makes permanent; control the quality of preparation – it will determine how you perform.

ATTENTION TO DETAIL

The practice of mental preparation is founded on attention to detail. When you give the little details the same treatment as the larger ones, you give yourself the most opportunities to employ techniques of the mental game. This applies not only to when you practice your sport, but to cultivating your mental preparation through daily actions representative of that preparation mentality. With the adoption of this lifestyle, the practice of mental conditioning becomes routine and this perspective becomes habit. Daily tasks become performance preparation. All the more reason to seize the day, and take PRIDE (Personal Responsibility In Daily Excellence) in your preparation.

PERFORMANCE INTENSITY

If you want to improve your performance in games, the best way to begin is to start increasing the intensity of your practices. This can be accomplished by increasing the tempo and pace in practice. As we learned from Coach Wooden at the beginning of the chapter, *the harder and faster you compete in practice, the more comfortable you feel in games.*

If you can make decisions and actions happen faster in practice than in games, you are giving yourself the best chance to play at your best against teams or players who have more talent. When you face these opponents, the pace of the game tends to speed up. If you practice under up-tempo conditions, you will be more capable of holding your own, because you will have established—mentally and physically—the endurance and stamina through your preparation.

Remember, tempo and pace are measured under time. Find ways you can use a stopwatch in practice to pick up the pace.

BE QUICK, BUT DO NOT HURRY

Yet, another one of Coach Wooden's great maxims was the advice, "Be quick, but do not hurry." This is significant because you want to increase the tempo of practice without compromising the quality of the practice. This is an important balancing act in your performance preparation. Work too fast, the more mistakes you will make and the less you improve your game. This rule is applicable to the development of both physical skills and mental skills.

Coach Wooden's advice, however, serves a warning to those who want to shortcut the process. Before you increase the intensity of performance, you should be proficient in the fundamental skills necessary for such performance. This seems intuitive, but when people hurry to play at the highest level, they often run headfirst into the brick wall of reality—the reality there is no shortcut to excellence. This is why it is important to make sure to practice technique before you increase tempo. It is good to be a quick study, but some things should not be rushed. Sometimes the best way to learn something is to take care and be methodical, and then steadily increase the pace of your practice.

In order to prepare for performance, you should push the pace in practice and make yourself uncomfortable. It is absolutely necessary to *learn how to be comfortable with being uncomfortable* if you want to perform at a level of excellence. It is important to practice a fast pace and quick tempo, but do not hurry your preparation.

THE "STEP UP" HAPPENS EVERY DAY

A lot of athletes say they will "step up their game" when they play their division rivals or that they will "step it up" in the big game. As a peak performance coach, this is both perplexing and insightful. It is perplexing because if you have the ability to "step up," why are you not bringing your best *whenever* you compete. It is simultaneously insightful because it shows the mentality of the player[s] saying this, illustrating an immature perspective towards performance. These players obviously do not understand the value of excellent preparation.

There is no "step up." If you can play at the highest level – as Nike's slogan states – just do it! There is no conceivable reason to not play at your best during competition; there isn't even a conceivable reason to do it in practice. As Michael Jordan says, "I play to win, whether during practice or a real game. And I will not let anything get in the way of me and my competitive enthusiasm to win." As His Airness would probably ask, why "step up" in the big game when it is what you should be doing every day in practice?

As we have discussed, performance reflects preparation. You will not maximize your potential if you pursue excellence only once in a while during practice sessions. If you wish to be a success, you must pursue excellence *all* the time. The "step up" happens – every day.

MEASUREMENT = MOTIVATION

Dave Serrano, the head baseball coach at University of California, Irvine from 2005-2007 and the current head baseball coach at the University of Tennessee, is a true master of the mental game. As head coach of the UCI Anteaters, Coach Serrano implemented mental conditioning as the foundation of the program. One of the keys to Coach Serrano's success with his team was his understanding that measurement equals motivation.

The best way to motivate yourself is to measure your progress. Simply believing that you will give your best without specific measurement of performance is unrealistic. Coach Serrano recognizes this and, with his attention to detail, he measures all the preparation of his team to motivate his players and to instill mental conditioning techniques. His simple utilization of a stopwatch is all it takes. By recording anything from the times run out of the batter's box to first base after a hit to the team's transitions from one drill to another, Coach Serrano gives his team measurements to gauge their daily efforts compared to their best times on record. In doing so, players on the team are held accountable for their efforts in their daily preparation, which makes the whole team practice harder and at a higher level on a consistent basis.

THE POWER OF TIME

During preparation, a stopwatch is the best accountability partner of a peak performer. The stopwatch is simple to use, unbiased, and blatantly honest about your performance effort. As the last section espoused, measurement equals motivation, and time is one of the great motivators in life. The utilization of a stopwatch is sure to motivate you to constantly improve your times, wherever appropriate, during your preparation routines.

The use of a stopwatch anywhere, from lifting weights to simulating competitive game time scenarios, will draw the excellence out of your performance. By pressuring players to accomplish game-like scenarios in a limited amount of time, if not a shorter time than in during competition, they will learn to cope with uncomfortable situations. This can be applied to baseball by timing how long it takes for the catcher to throw the ball to second in a stolen base simulation; or for increasing the intensity of a press in basketball by giving the in bounding team seven seconds to pass half court as opposed to ten. Ultimately, this forces players to work faster than they normally would if there was no stopwatch, and as fast or faster, than they will need to in a game.

The power of time can be applied through the use of a stopwatch in any sport. Utilizing a stopwatch in your performance preparation will immediately increase the game-like speed, intensity, and tempo while you practice. You will also learn to cope with pressure and feel comfortable with uncomfortable situations, because *on the edge of discomfort is where learning takes place.* Think about how you can implement a stopwatch in your preparation to help create an environment of pressure and discomfort to enhance your performance development. By keeping track of time and pushing yourself, the game will reward you for your efforts in your competitive performance.

ACTION STEP: What can you measure to make your preparation process more competitive and to make you work faster then you might have to in a game?

1) _____

2) _____

3) _____

RECORD PROGRESS

One of the most effective methods to measure performance improvement is to regularly record your progress in a peak performance journal. When athletes take the initiative to record the details of their progress in a journal of some kind, they hold themselves accountable for their preparation. Such a journal can be used, to keep quantifiable measurements of preparation drills, help to remove the emotions from daily preparation, and record factual assessments. It can also can also be used to record reflections of daily performance, helping to understand how your feelings that day effect your it.

For each day of performance preparation, write down times, important lessons, areas in need of improvement, a goal for the next day based off today's practice session, and anything else that applies to your performance. Recording progress grants the opportunity to apply the three steps of performance change. It enables you to reflect on the information you record, generates awareness of areas of improvement, and enables you to create and implement new strategies for performance development. When you know what giving your best is and it is on record, you can better judge your effort with objectivity. This speeds up the learning and the improvement processes. In sum, when you record progress, you make record progress.

THE PEAK PERFORMANCE SPORT JOURNAL

One of the most beneficial routine exercises someone in the pursuit of excellence can do is keep a peak performance journal. The peak performance journal is a tool to help you further develop your mental skills for peak performance. Remember, you must be in control of yourself before you can control your performance. The first step in gaining self-control is to develop an awareness of your performance, so that you can recognize when you are distracted from the present moment and the most appropriate mental state for success.

DEVELOP AWARENESS

Developing awareness is the first step towards consistent levels of performance. Remember the three steps to performance change: (1) Awareness, (2) Strategy, (3) Implementation of the Strategy. This journal provides you with an opportunity to record the different strategies you are working on to maintain and regain self-control.

GET IT OUT OF YOUR HEAD AND ON PAPER

The long-range goal is to develop various strategies you can implement in stressful situations to help you perform at your best when it means the most. If you choose to, the journal also can be a place where you can record your feelings and the personal knowledge that you are gaining about yourself, the game, your teammates, and any other factors. This is one of the few times in your life that you will ever direct so much energy toward one specific goal. There is a lot to learn from your pursuit of excellence. This journal will give you something to reflect on after your high-level participation is completed.

The journal also can serve as a place where you can express your feelings in writing or drawings. It is beneficial to get these feelings out in some way so that they do not build up and lead to unproductive tension. The use of colored pens is often helpful to express yourself, even if you are not an artist. Research has shown this strategy to be a beneficial stress-management technique.

CREATE A ROUTINE FOR WRITING

You do not have to make an entry every day, but should strive to be consistent in your writing routine. Remember, to be successful you must be able to describe what you do as a process/routine. So make your journal entries as routine as possible. Making your entries at the same time of day is a great way to formulate your journal writing routine.

The journal is an informal record of your thoughts and experiences as you train for high-level performance. If you choose to have someone read your journal, please feel free to delete any parts that you think are too personal to share. The objective for someone who is reviewing your writing should be to guide you and to make suggestions that may facilitate your self-exploration in reaching your goals.

I highly recommend that you try the peak performance journal as a strategy to learn about yourself and speed up your learning curve. Remember, it's the start that stops most people, so commit to it for the next 2-3 weeks and feel free to write whatever comes to your mind. The following section includes suggestions with accompanying questions/ descriptors that can help guide your entries. As with all things, you will become more comfortable with the journal process as you develop a routine over time.

SAMPLE QUESTIONS TO WRITE ABOUT

1. Peak Performance: What does it feel like when you play and/or practice at your best? Describe some of your most enjoyable experiences playing your sport. What have you learned from these moments when you are playing at your best?

2. Stressors: Write down your thoughts about various events outside your sport that are distracting to you. For example, parents, boy/girlfriends, peers, job hassles, financial issues, community (home-town expectations). Do the same for distractions on the field, such as importance of contest, location, spectators, etc.

3. Coaching Style: What do you need from your coaches? How can you best help them help you reach your goals? What can you do to make your relationship with your coaches more productive?

4. Teammates: What do you want from your teammates? What can you give them? How do you relate and work with your teammates? Write about your relationship with other teammates. Any unfinished business you need to work through?

5. Confidence: At this time, how confident are you in regard to achieving your goals? What can you do differently to feel more confident? What can you ask of yourself, coach, and/ or teammates?

6. Manifestations of Your Stress: How do you experience high levels of anxiety in performance? Assess your thoughts, physiological and behavioral reactions. What strategies did you use to help intervene with your stress and keep balance?

7. Awareness and Concentration: What changes do you observe in your performance when you are aware? What concentration methods are you experimenting with? What are your focal points for various skills?

TRUST YOUR PREPARATION

Preparation is everything to a peak performer. It is taking all the elements necessary to performance excellence and practicing them tirelessly and with a relentless energy to achieve progress. As you read through this manual, integrate all the material into your preparation. The constant practice of mental conditioning with your physical conditioning is of utmost significance to reaching the pinnacle of performance excellence. As the great master of preparation, Coach John Wooden, used to say, "Failing to prepare is preparing to fail."

Most importantly, trust your preparation. Placing trust in your performance preparation and taking pride in the fact that you are doing things the right way will make all the difference in your journey. The climb up The Mountain of Excellence will undoubtedly be treacherous at times, but if you trust that you have prepared at a consistent effort of excellence, your preparation is bound to reward you.

CHAPTER #7 REVIEW

- "Nothing is better for intense game pressure than countless hours of disciplined effort spent mastering the fundamentals." – Coach John Wooden

- Repetition alone does not bring rewards; it is the quality that matters.

- Rewarded behavior becomes repeated behavior.

- Make practices competitive.

- Utilize a process-based scoring system to reward desired performance.

- Extra efforts give you the competitive advantage.

- Practice does not make perfect, practice makes permanent.

- Attention to details makes the difference.

- "Be quick, but do not hurry." – Coach John Wooden

- You must learn to be comfortable with being uncomfortable.

- The "step up" happens every day.

- Measurement equals motivation; you treasure what you measure.

- A stopwatch is a great motivator and accountability partner.

- When you record progress, you make record progress.

- "Failing to prepare is preparing to fail."
  – Coach John Wooden

NOTES:

NOTES:

NOTES:

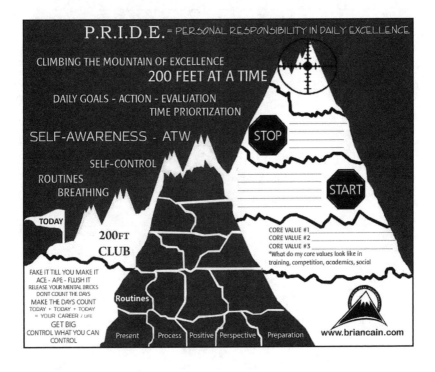

CHAPTER #8

The secrets of success are hidden in the routines of our daily lives. You can know all the information within the previous chapters, but if you do not implement this information, then what good does it do for you? The purpose of any routine is to augment performance. Routines are effective at this because they give structure by providing a consistent starting point to activate a regular procedure. In sports, a consistent frame of reference is essential to performance excellence by providing the mind and body a sense of security even under conditions that remain out of your control. The familiarity of routines establishes good performance habits and your investment in cultivating them will pay big dividends on your pursuit of excellence.

This chapter will explore routines that will implement the information you learned in the previous chapters. This chapter will discuss routines that keep you in the present moment and focused on the process, routines that give you the necessary perspective to maintain a positive mentality, and routines to establish during your preparation placing you in a position for performance excellence.

PRE-GAME & POST-GAME ROUTINES

Pre-game and post-game routines are important for all athletes to develop. The purpose of these routines is to transform your mentality from your "real-self" to your "performing-self" and vice versa. In Chapter 5, we discussed how to facilitate this self-transformation through the practice of segmentation and later in this chapter I'll give you some specific methods to implement in your own routines.

Most athletes have pre-game routines. Some individual pre-game routines I've witnessed range from players listening to a particular song or playlist, putting on their uniforms in a particular order, doing a certain set of stretches, and leaving the team to do mental imagery in silence for a couple minutes in solitude, just to name a few. Teams also have rituals before going out to perform in games, whether they are team warm-ups, team meetings/huddles, or team chants. The purpose of these routines is to make you feel comfortable by giving you a sense of familiarity, while transforming you into your competitive mentality.

Post-game routines are a system of steps that allow the athlete to decompress after competition. Most athletes' post-game routines consist of having a brief post-game meeting with their coach or team, taking off their uniforms, cleaning themselves up, getting dressed, and calling it a day. Post-game routines, however, have the potential to be so much more significant than this "going-through-the-motions" process. Later in this mission you'll learn how to create a post-game routine that enhances your pursuit of post-performance excellence.

IN-GAME ROUTINES

An in-game routine provides the performer with a set of mental checkpoints. Golfers standing over putts, tennis players bouncing the ball before serve, hitters stepping into the batter's box, pitchers stepping on the pitching rubber, and basketball players taking a certain number of dribbles at the free-throw line are just some of the many in-game routines performed in sports. By going through a series of mental checkpoints, athletes place themselves in the present moment and focus on the process at hand. In the heat of competition, these routines serve as a chance for athletes to control themselves and their performances.

Make sure that your coaches and teammates are aware of your in-game routines. This is important because they can act as accountability partners during performance and can remind you to check back into your routines if you are in a funk. You should also learn the in-game routines of your teammates so you can return their focus on a familiar frame of reference. In-game routines are imperative to self-control, giving you the best opportunity to execute with performance excellence.

CIRCLE OF FOCUS

Inside of your in-competition routine, you step into your circle of focus. The circle of focus is an imaginary circle that you step into and engage in a present moment focus with your energy and attention going out towards the action taking place. For example, the shortstop in softball steps into her circle of focus as the pitcher gets ready to throw; the receiving team steps into its circle of focus as the opposing volleyball team gets ready to serve. Stepping into this metaphorical circle of focus is a critical part of the in-competition routine in which you get into the present.

As part of the in-competition routine, you want to use one to three mental strategies to keep your focus locked into the present.

1) Deep breath on a focal point

2) Visualize – Mental Imagery

3) Verbalize – Self-Talk of Final Thought

CAIN'S COACHING POINT:
Because I cannot see if the athlete is doing mental imagery and I cannot see if the athlete is using their final thought, as a coach, I want my athletes to take a deep breath each pitch so I can see that they are in-control of themselves, .

These strategies will assist your focus on performing in the present moment and places the routine use of one or more of these strategies to help you enter that circle of focus and gain control of your mind. Mind control leads to body control, which leads to performance control, and being in control of all aspects of yourself, gives you the best chance for performance excellence.

VERBALIZING YOUR FINAL THOUGHT

We have discussed how all athletes use self-talk during performance, and an athlete's final thought builds upon the self-talk concept in a more play-specific manner. As discussed in the Chapter 5, the final thought is the last thought in an athlete's mind before performing a specific aspect of the game. Before making a play, you want to think to yourself a particular positive phrase that intensifies your focus on the accomplishment of that play. You want to integrate this final thought into your performance routine to augment the mind-body performance connection. Mentally conditioning a final thought will establish a routine rhythm to your performance, giving you the best opportunity for performance excellence.

In baseball, internally verbalizing your final thought has also been called having a swing thought or a pitch thought. There is a significant difference between being in the batter's box and telling yourself, "Drive it! Drive it! Drive it!" versus, "Do not strike out. I have to get a hit." Your final thought will make a big difference in your performance because a positive and aggressive final thought will give you the best chance to follow through in your performance. The same holds true for a basketball, soccer, or hockey player's shot thought, a volleyball or tennis player's serve thought, or a football player's tackle thought.

DRILLS FOR FINAL THOUGHTS

Practicing final thoughts is important to maximize their effectiveness on a routine basis. With the baseball teams I work with, I set up a soft toss or batting tee and have the players verbalize their final swing thoughts out loud. I have the hitter tell me their swing thought out loud and I listen, as well as, watch the rhythm of their mechanics. Out loud, they are saying their final thought of, "Drive it! Drive it! Drive it!" They load on the pitch and then swing. We take three swings with the verbalization of the final thought, so I can hear what their final thought is and see them using it with the rhythm of their body. The same kind of drills can be performed for shooting in basketball, spiking in volleyball, slapshots in hockey, serves in tennis, punches in boxing, tackles in football, etc.

 To see a video of a drill in which an athlete uses a final thought, please visit www.MentalConditioningManual.com/extras

As a teammate, if you know a teammate's final thought, then during the game give them positive encouragement. If their swing thought is "Drive it," then you might say, "Let's drive it right here!" after a missed swing to help get that player refocused on his final thought.

Peak performers also utilize mental imagery as a component of their performance routines. The use of mental imagery is an excellent way to psychologically prepare yourself for performance by visualizing yourself executing a specific performance task within your sport. Chapter 12 is devoted to the significance of mental imagery for peak performance.

SUPERMAN SEGMENTATION & SEPARATION

As you learned in Chapter 6, segmentation routines are used to help separate yourself from the many different hats you wear. If you are reading this and you are a college or high school athlete, you have school, social activities, and sport to separate in your life, while if you are a professional, you have at least the latter two. Inside of those different aspects of your life, you may wear the hat of son or daughter, brother or sister, significant other, friend, etc. One of the best techniques to help segment and separate the many hats you wear is to use something physical (perhaps a hat!) to help you change your mental state. It is here we look to Superman for guidance.

Superman is the ultimate pro at segmentation and separation prior to and after his performances. He walks into the phone booth as Clark Kent, super-nerd, and comes out as Superman, superhero. His self-transformative process is the perfect example for peak performance segmentation routines. The nearest phone booth is the symbolic equivalent of his locker room and as he changes his clothes, so does his perspective, as he adopts a peak performance mentality. One college athletic team I worked with took this principle so far as to get a superman logo for the outside of their locker room door to serve as a reminder that when you walked into the locker room to change your clothes, you were also changing your mentality from student (Clark Kent) to athlete (Superman).

Select the clothes that epitomize your self-transformative process. As you take off each item or put it on, think about the transformation taking place and the necessary change in mentality. Release the mental bricks from your personal life as you get into your performance mentality, or release the mental bricks of your performance as you return yourself to your personal life. Changing your clothes is a process to help you separate the mentality you need to succeed in the various segments of your life, by breaking down the process into various segments. The establishment of these routines gives you the best chance to be in the present, whatever you are about to perform.

MOVE THROUGH THE HOURGLASS

 Another way to think about the process of segmentation and separation is to imagine an hourglass as a visual example of how your pre-performance and post-performance routines will work. The shape of the hourglass reflects the segmentation and separation process, with a definite start point (top of the hour glass) and end point (bottom of the hourglass) with a defined middle section. This hourglass shape mirrors the self-transformative routine because you begin the process as either your "real-self" or "performing-self" and end as the opposite. The hourglass transformation is marked by some physical routine actions such as changing clothes, where you strip down from, say, your casual clothes to your team uniform. When you are naked during the process of changing, you are in the middle of that transformative process—the middle of the hourglass.

Changing your clothes is common routine for segmentation and separation, but a number of other routines, such as turning off the cell phone or taking a shower, can also mark the self-transformation.

CAIN'S COACHING POINT:
I suggest using your cellphone as a tool to help you transform yourself and as a reminder to stay in the present moment. When you turn off your cell phone, it is a sign that you are shifting your mentality from student to athlete, and that you are letting go of the academics, social media, significant other, friends, family and other potential distractions that could keep you from being the ultimate athlete. When that cell phone goes off, you are going to feel yourself moving through your mental hourglass and becoming a peak performer.

The athletes I work with hardly ever turn their cell phones off, so when you do, that means you are going to be doing something special. You have got to treat practice and games like they are special opportunities for development, because they are. Let nothing outside of your sport interfere with mentally preparing for performance.

CAIN'S COACHING POINT:
If you are a coach, I suggest you get your team practice uniforms; something as simple as the same T-shirt and/or shorts. This will help your athletes with the segmentation purposes as they will have a uniform they change into. You will teach them the importance of the mindset that they need to have when that uniform is on. Invest the time to educate them on the importance of changing the clothes and changing the mindset to get present.

After you turn your cell phone off, you then start the changing-of-your-clothes process. As you take off your shirt, let go of the test you failed. As you take off your pants, let go of the person who cut you off on your drive into practice. As you take off your shoes, there go the issues you are having at home. As you physically change your clothes, you are ridding yourself of all that mental baggage and turning yourself into the ultimate athlete. As you move toward the middle of the hourglass, you become fully present and fully focused on what you plan to accomplish today.

Then, as you put on your performance gear, you begin to emerge on the other end of the hourglass. As you begin putting on your uniform, you feel yourself getting more energized and more focused. As you lace up your sneakers, you feel locked in and prepared to perform to the best of your abilities, striving for performance excellence. Finally, you come out on the other end of the hourglass, mentally prepared to DOMINATE THE DAY! By following this hourglass segmentation and separation routine you are setting the stage for a quality performance.

TENNESSEE ORANGE LINE

Rod Delmonico is the former head baseball coach at the University of Tennessee. When I worked with him in 2007, he painted an orange line separating the Volunteers clubhouse and the dugout. He instructed his players that when they crossed that orange line the only thing that mattered was Tennessee Baseball. He coached his players to use that line as the last bit of their routine to help segment between their student/social self (real-self) and their baseball self (performing-self).

THE GLADIATOR IS READY FOR BATTLE

The last thing you do before performance should be part of a physical routine to signal you are ready to perform. One of the best illustrations of this is in the movie *Gladiator*, when Maximus (Russell Crowe) reaches down for a bit of earth to rub between his hands and then throws the remnants back to the ground. This is his pre-game routine symbolizing he has gathered his battle mentality. It is a sign that Maximus is in the present moment, nothing can distract his focus, and he is ready to perform in war.

Develop your own pre-game routine to collect your performance mentality. I often suggest that you take a moment and retie your shoes to check into your performance state of mind. By doing this, you lace it up, and lock it in. LeBron James powders his hands and tosses the remnants in the air, in an act similar to that of Maximus. Whatever the physical act may be, use it to activate your performance mentality and enter your circle of focus. Let yourself know that you are Gladiator ready.

FOCAL POINTS

Whenever you perform, it is important to have and utilize focal points. Focal points are mental check points that you go to throughout your journey up The Mountain of Excellence as a part of your in-competition routine. You check in on your mental and emotional state and, when necessary, bring yourself back into the present moment. The basketball player could use a banner in the gym that he look at and takes a deep breath each time someone goes to the foul line for two shots. This technique allows players to have a routine in which they are able to look at their focal point, take a deep breath, and get back to a calm, focused, and centered place in the present.

Batters in baseball or softball will often use a spot on their bat or on home plate. Pitchers will often look at the corner of the pitching rubber or the toe of their shoe as a focal point. Hockey players often use a spot on their stick or a shoelace on their skates. Tennis players use an intersection of their strings or a spot on the racket. Mix martial artists will use a spot on the canvas beneath their feet such as the Harley Davidson sign or the trademark ® which, for them, symbolically means READY and signals to gain control of oneself. The routine use of a focal point and a deep breath will put you in control of yourself and in a better place mentally and physically, giving you the best chance for success.

ACTION STEP: What is a focal point you can use at your practice field to help you regain control?

TAKE A DEEP BREATH

The deep breath is an important part of any performance routine, because the breath connects you to the present moment. Taking a deep breath pulls you right back to the"'here" and the "now". The deep breath brings oxygen into your system, slows down your heart rate, clears your mental state and puts you back in control of yourself.

 ACTION STEP: In your sport, when is there a break in the action where you can take a deep breath and re-center yourself?

As a baseball/softball coach, I want to see my players breathe between each pitch, so I have a visual reference point to identify how my players are feeling and where they are at mentally. It enables me to recognize when players are letting the game speed up on them and helps them settle back down. In pressure situations, often the first thing to break down will be your routine. Once you lose your routine, next goes your mind control, and your loss of physical performance is right around the corner. Make sure to take your deep breaths during performance to keep your head in YOUR game.

ROUTINE PERFORMANCE REVIEW

A routine review of your most recent performance is one of the best post-game routines you can establish on your pursuit of performance excellence. Keeping a peak performance journal chronicles your progress and development in your mental and physical conditioning, providing you with a valuable resource for self-improvement. This gives you the ability to reflect upon past performances and recall how you performed, how you were feeling, what you believe you need to improve, what performance adjustments you must make, whether or not past performance adjustments worked, etc. In the previous chapter, I addressed how recorded progress becomes record progress, and making the act of recording performance routines is the first step in the right direction.

The best time to integrate this performance routine review is directly after performance, while your performance is fresh in your mind. Record all the information about your performance that is applicable to the improvement of your performance. As you push yourself to excellence, challenge yourself to become better by being self-critical and not being merely content with a solid performance. Make sure, however, that you also give some focus to what you did well during your performance. Doing this will serve as a reminder to you to continue performing these aspects of the game and will enable you to catch yourself if those aspects of your game start slipping. This is all invaluable information for developing your performance to become a peak performer.

MAKE IT ROUTINE

A routine is a skill that needs to be practiced regularly, so that it becomes, well, routine. You cannot just do a routine once and expect to have it show up for you in the heat of the competitive arena. The routine has to be something you do on a daily basis in practice. Game-like practice is critical to your mental game development because it enhances your ability to stick to your routines in pressure situations. Ultimately, the purpose of routines is to provide something physical to assist us with something mental.

Remember, *practice makes permanent.* You want to drill these routines during your preparation, making it such a permanent part of your performance process that you unconsciously tune into a predetermined mindset for performance excellence. It is also worth noting, you should approach your routine in the same manner you approach the entire performance: with quality effort, attention to detail, and present moment focus on the process. Breaking down all elements of your performance into routines will ultimately make it a routine performance and give you the structure within your performance that will enable you to develop performance excellence. Making performance skills routine, ultimately makes the experience of climbing The Mountain of Excellence feel much simpler.

 For a sample routine check list, please visit www.MentalConditioningManual.com/extras

CHAPTER #8 REVIEW

- **The secrets of success are hidden in the routines of our daily lives.**

- **Pre-game and post-game routines are important to get yourself into and out of your performance mentality.**

- **In-game routines enhance self-control.**

- **Step into your circle of focus during performance.**

- **Establish a final thought for performance tasks.**

- **Superman used segmentation and separation techniques and so should you.**

- **Move through the hourglass for performance self-transformation.**

- **Lace it up and lock it in to be Gladiator ready.**

- **During performance, use focal points to mentally check in.**

- **Integrate taking a deep breath into your performance routines.**

- **Performance routines must be regularly practiced to maximize their potentials.**

NOTES:

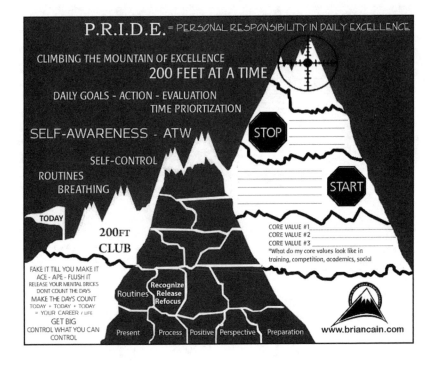

CHAPTER #9
RECOGNIZE, RELEASE, REFOCUS

Recognizing your physical, emotional, and mental state within the context of your competitive environment is critical to staying in control of yourself, thereby giving yourself the best opportunity to achieve performance excellence. The development of mental methods for recognition, release, and refocus are essential to peak performance, and understanding the process of maintenance is required to achieve an excellent competitive mentality. This chapter will give you the skills to develop your own maintenance system to keep your state of mind active and engaged in the journey up The Mountain of Excellence.

RECOGNIZING YOUR SIGNAL LIGHTS

The most challenging aspect of the mental game is learning to recognize when your performance is taking a turn for the worse and then developing a system to make the necessary corrections to return to performance excellence. The recognition that you are having a performance breakdown is the primary and most crucial step in this process. Recognizing where you are – mentally, emotionally, and physically – is called your ATW (Awareness To Win). Nobody is perfect. Every athlete loses control of themselves on occasion, but it is the athlete who can correct himself the quickest who tends to perform consistently and, ultimately, has more success.

SIGNAL LIGHTS EXPLAINED

If you are driving a car and you come to a green light, you would naturally proceed forward. If you are driving a car and the light turns yellow, some of us would slow down while some of us would speed up, depending on where we are in relation to the light. When you come to a red light, however, you must stop or you are going to crash and burn. Now, if you are reading this chuckling to yourself about the time you ran a red light and didn't cause an accident or get caught by the police, then I caution against such complacency. Maybe you won't crash and burn every time, but make this reckless and unlawful action a habit, and it is bound to catch up with you.

"DON'T RUN THROUGH RED LIGHTS"

Performance awareness is similar to driving a car on the road. When you have green lights (positive, confident, specific, and aggressive thoughts and feelings) you are in control of yourself. In performance, you encounter yellow lights (hopeful, uncertain, vague, and timid thoughts and feelings), which occur when something negative happens to take you out of a green light mentality. If your yellow lights are not recognized and that adversity is not addressed, then you will often find yourself in red lights (negative, dejected, apathetic, and destructive thoughts and feelings).

The easiest way for you to think about your signal lights is:

Green – You are giving yourself the best opportunity for performance excellence.

Yellow – You are starting to lose the mentality conducive to peak performance.

Red – You are totally out of control and it is reflecting in your performance.

The goal of all peak performers is to hike up The Mountain of Excellence with green lights as much as possible, while your head lamp focuses on the next 200 feet of the journey.

CAUSES OF YELLOW & RED LIGHTS

Removal from your green light mentality could be caused by any number of adverse situations. Yellow and red lights could result from making a mistake, an official making a bad call, a coach's criticism, fans getting on your nerves, your opponent talking trash, or any number of other things that can become stuck in your head. Adversity comes in all forms, physical and mental, and does not have to involve events within your performance environment. The world outside of your performance arena also can affect your performance if you are not in control of yourself. These might include that grudge against your boss, the schoolwork you must accomplish, or your latest love interest. Do not let these things distract you from your present moment focus and peak performance mentality. Focusing on what you are trying to avoid, instead of what you are trying to accomplish, is a recipe for disastrous performance.

LESSONS FROM MMA

 If you are a mixed martial arts fighter, red lights could be a fighter who has badly beaten you in the past or facing someone you have idolized your whole career. It could be an overwhelming amount of self-doubt when you get inside the cage wondering whether you have done everything necessary to prepare, or thinking that if you lose your career will be over.

Mixed martial arts is an amazing sport when it comes to fighters getting trapped by their red lights and not having the skills to deal with them. I have worked with a lot of fighters, and almost all say, they have lost a fight before it started, because they were in red lights and did not recognize it, or recognized it, and did not have a reliable mental maintenance system to help them get back to green. In mixed martial arts you can train for six to ten weeks for a fifteen-minute fight, and if you step in the Octagon with the mindset of fighting not to lose, as opposed to fighting to win, then you will likely lose.

In any sport, if your mind is illuminated by the red lights of a negative mentality, you are nearly guaranteed to be on the losing end of your competition. Focusing on what you are trying to avoid, instead of what you are trying to accomplish, is a recipe for disastrous performance in the cage and in life.

THREE WAYS TO RECOGNIZE YOUR SIGNAL LIGHTS

There are three major areas in which you can develop

your performance awareness and learn to better recognize your signal lights. The three areas in which you can often recognize where you are at mentally, physically, and emotionally are:

1. Self-talk – What you are saying to yourself.

2. Physical feelings – How you are feeling, physically.

3. Situations – Circumstances which arise in performance that will trigger particular signal lights.

CAIN'S COACHING POINT: The purpose of routines is to maintain self-control and get into a green light performance mentality as often as possible.

GREEN LIGHTS

Green lights are an easy concept to comprehend. They represent the mentality of peak performance; where you are feeling positive, aggressive, and confident; focused on the present process at hand; and in control of your performance thoughts and actions. Green lights are performance movers and confidence builders. One athlete I worked with referred to the green light mentality as the CAT mentality – Confident, Aggressive and Tough. When you are confident, aggressive, and tough, you are locked into the moment and moving forward with green lights. By staying in the green light, you give yourself the best opportunity to have an excellent performance.

In order to recognize when you are not in a green light state of mind, you must first recognize what signs indicate that you are in the green. The next three sections will help you use the three major areas of signal light recognition to identify your green light mentality.

GREEN LIGHTS – SELF-TALK

When you have green lights, what are you saying to yourself?

Some examples could be:

1. You cannot touch me.

2. I am feeling it; so they better bring it.

3. I own this gym; this is my house.

4. Yes sir, I am too good.

Green light thoughts are much like your confidence conditioning statements but shorter and very specific to your athletic performance. They are usually aggressive, external, specific, and confident thoughts.

ACTION STEP: Write down your green light thoughts – what you say to yourself when you are playing at your best.

_____

_____

_____

_____

GREEN LIGHTS – PHYSICAL FEELINGS

When you have green lights, how do you feel physically?

Most athletes will report:

1. I feel light on my feet.

2. My muscles are relaxed and I have good energy.

3. I feel strong and I have big body language.

ACTION STEP: Write down your green light feelings – how you feel physically when you are playing at your best.

_____

_____

_____

_____

_____

GREEN LIGHT - SITUATIONS

What situations or actions in competition, practice, the weight room, or academic settings put you into green lights?

Most performers will report:

1. When I have a great warm-up.

2. When I have had a good night's sleep.

3. When I practiced my presentation over and over, so I knew the content forward and backward.

4. When I stick with my routine.

 ACTION STEP: Write down the situations in performance that will place you into your green light – the situations where you know you will play at your best.

_____

_____

_____

_____

_____

_____

RED & YELLOW LIGHTS

Athletes I have worked with in the past have occasionally become caught up on trying to identify whether they were in a red light or yellow light. As an athlete, I want you not to get hung up on that distinction because it is counterproductive to peak performance. This distinction is more relevent for coaches because they must discern which measure will help you get back into your green light mentality – telling you to take a deep breath, calling a timeout, or making a substitution.

As an athlete, the distinction does not matter as much. Red lights are negative thoughts, and confidence cutters, and performance stoppers, and yellow leads you there. Green is where you want to be. All you need to identify is whether or not you are giving yourself the green light. If you are not in the green, then recognize, release, and refocus on the performance at hand. The next three sections will help you use the three major areas of signal light recognition to identify whether you are in red/yellow lights.

RED/YELLOW/LIGHTS – SELF-TALK

When you have red/yellow lights, what are you saying to yourself?

Most athletes report:

1. I cannot believe the official made that call.

2. Why is coach saying that?

3. That player at the scorer's table is probably for me?

4. Why can I not hit anything.

5. Why do I play this stupid game?

6. I suck.

ACTION STEP: Write down your red/yellow light thoughts – what you say to yourself when you are struggling in your sport.284

_____

_____

_____

RED/YELLOW LIGHTS – PHYSICAL FEELINGS

When you have red/yellow lights, how do you feel physically?

Most athletes will report:

1. I do not feel good; I feel tired and slow.

2. I feel like I cannot catch my breath.

3. The bat feels like it is twice as heavy as it should be.

4. The ball feels like a foreign object.

5. I feel like the game's speeding up on me.

ACTION STEP: Write down your red/yellow light feelings – how you feel physically when you are playing below your potential.

_____

_____

_____

_____

RED /YELLOW LIGHT - SITUATIONS

What situations or actions in competition, practice, the weight room, or academic settings put you into red/yellow lights?

Most athletes will report:

1. When I fail to execute a play.

2. When an official makes bad call.

3. When a teammate makes a potentially costly error.

4. When I know I could have prepared better.

 ACTION STEP: Write down what situations in performance will put you into a red/yellow light and what happens when you are playing at your worst and removes you from your green light mentality.

_____

_____

_____

_____

_____

SIGNAL LIGHTS = PERFORMANCE CHANGE

Once you have identified your self-talk, your physical feelings, and the situations that put you into your green and red/yellow lights, you immediately give yourself a better chance to recognize your signal lights in performance. If you have green lights, refocus on the next play. If you have red/yellow lights, you must release before you refocus.

Remember the three steps to performance change:

1. Develop awareness of what needs to change.

2. Develop a strategy for change to happen.

3. Put that strategy into action.

Most athletes do not know how to make necessary performance adjustments because they have not developed performance awareness. Performance change is all about understanding your internal signal lights. Mentally, *what you are aware of you can control; what you are unaware of is going to control you.* This is why understanding and practicing the signal lights concept gives you the best opportunity to effectively exercise the three steps of performance change.

INVERTED U OF SIGNAL LIGHTS

Peak Performance 101 is about understanding the Inverted U. On the North-South axis, we have performance and on the East-West axis, intensity or focus. How excited are you? When you are not intense or focused enough, performance is low. Conversely, when you are over-intense or are too focused and trying to hard performance is still low. This is why it is important for peak performers to maintain a consistent mental state of excellence to compete with optimal energy and perform at their best 90% of the time.

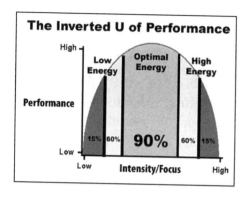

This mental state of performance excellence is maintained through the adoption of performance routines that create a maintenance system. What a mental maintenance routine does is take you from falling anywhere on the inverted U, and gives you a much better chance of consistently falling in the center, which is your optimal energy and arousal area for a peak performance. This routine-based mental maintenance system gives you the best chance of performing at the peak of the Inverted U.

PERFORMANCE ROUTINES

Performance routines are the life jacket of peak performance. As you learned in Chapter 8, when the pressure is on you turn to your routines so that you can stay in the present moment and increase your chances of achieving performance excellence. The importance of routines to performance is a simple formula: routines lead to consistency, consistency leads to confidence, and confidence leads to success.

CAIN'S COACHING POINT: To be consistent over time, you must be able to describe what you do, your routine, as a process.

The best programs I have been around have specific systems and structured performance routines that help players perform consistently over time. These programs often stress the importance of having a focal point to turn to during pressure performances. When you get distracted, or you have red/yellow light thoughts and start beating yourself up, your focal point is your box of positive thoughts and represents your check point helping you slow down and get back into your green lights.

RELEASE

Once you have learned to recognize your signal lights, the next step in the process is developing a release routine. The purpose of your release is to have a physical routine to help you get back in control of yourself and back into your green lights. This release routine facilitates your transition back to a green light mentality. When you are in red/yellow lights, *you must develop some sort of physical routine to help you mentally release the negative frustration*. This physical action should be an expressive release to collect control of your mental state and return you to the pursuit of performance excellence.

ACTION STEP: Examples of common releases are to clap your hands, take a deep breath, or undo and redo part of your equipment such as a chin strap or batting gloves. What are physical releases you can use to help you get from red/yellow lights and back to green?

1) _____

2) _____

3) _____

RELEASE YOUR MENTAL BRICKS

 At one point or another, we all make errors and mistakes. There is a common tendency to continue to carry these mistakes and poor performances, resulting in a buildup of negative mental energy. Instead of beating yourself up over a poor performance, you must learn to release these "mental bricks" that weigh on your mind.

If every time you make a mistake, you were to grab a physical brick and carry that brick with you, it would weigh you down both physically and mentally. This would invariably inhibit you from performing to the best of your ability.

Now, visualize a mistake you are bitter about as a mental brick. When you carry this mistake with you, this mental brick, it takes the same toll as carrying a physical brick. The difference is you cannot see it because it is a weight within your mind.

In your quest for excellence, you must train yourself to release the mental bricks that threaten to weigh you down. This relies on a process of reflection and realization followed by the release. After a mistake or a poor performance, you must thoughtfully reflect on the experience and consider how you can improve. Once you have realized what improvements can be made in your performance, you can then release the error from your consciousness and move forward up The Mountain of Excellence.

 Visit www.MentalCondtioningManual.com/extras to learn more about releasing mental bricks.

EXAMPLES OF IN-COMPETITION RELEASES

In-competition releases will be varying for every sport. All releases, however, should be directed at a consistent focal point. Your focal point could be an object in your performance arena, a team sign that is been hung up, or a part of your uniform. Whatever that focal point may be, when you look at it you should take a good deep breath, push out your chest, get big, and put all of that red/yellow light, negative energy and self-doubt into that sign. As you transfer that energy, remind yourself to get back to WIN (What's Important Now) and return to your green light thoughts and green light/refocus routine.

As a pitcher, you could take your foot and wipe off the rubber. Cleaning the rubber is symbolic of cleaning the slate. This physical action allows you to make a mental connection to the next pitch. I've got a new rubber, a new slate, it is clean, and I am ready to pitch.

Hitters can swipe the batter's box, get rid of old footprints, and in the process, get rid of the last pitch. They can then focus on their routine and playing the next pitch.

Here are some more examples of release routines:

You can shake your hands to shake off the red/yellow light thoughts.

You can make a fist, and as you release your fingers, release the past play.

You can clap your hands together and move on to the next play.

You can spit the red/yellow lights away.

There are hundreds of different releases you can use. The important part of the release is to be sure that you are taking a deep breath and have a focal point as a part of your release. As long as you establish a release routine with these two elements when you recognize you have lost your green light mentality, you have complete creative liberty.

FLUSH IT

A fun way to think about releasing mental bricks is by conjuring the image of a toilet. When you have a mental brick that is in danger of putting you in red lights, you want to take this mental brick and "flush it." Once you are relieved of that mental brick, you are ready to return to the present moment in your performance.

University of Vermont Hockey Head Coach Kevin Sneddon took this concept and integrated it into part of his team's post-performance routine. He keeps a miniature foam toilet in the team dressing room, and after a frustrating period or a hard-fought game, he and his players will flush the mental bricks from their performance. "I ask each of my players to flush the game down the toilet and move on," says Coach Sneddon. "The visual works quite well."

Visit www.MentalConditioningManual.com/extras to learn more about how the UVM Hockey Team uses the foam toilet to "Flush It."

It is inevitable that, as you climb The Mountain of Excellence, you will face forms of adversity that weigh on your mind. Do not carry these mental bricks with you on your journey. Stop routinely at your mental toilet to relieve yourself of their weight. Perform your release routine to flush away the negativity built within those mental bricks. Your mind will feel lighter, clearer, and be more mentally agile when you get back to your climb.

REFOCUS

Once you recognize your signal lights and release your red/ yellow lights with your release routine, it becomes critical that you refocus back into the present moment. Refocusing returns your mind to your WIN (What's Important Now) mentality and pushes you towards performance excellence. One of the best ways you can refocus is to talk out loud with your teammates during competition. When you talk out loud, you are external and present. When you are quiet, you can easily get lost in your own head, thinking about the past or the future. Refocus back to the present moment and you will give yourself the best chance to perform at your best.

SO WHAT, NEXT PITCH! MENTALITY

Refocusing, just like all mental conditioning, requires that your mind and body work together. If your body is trying to play the game in the moment, and your mind is still analyzing a previous play or thinking about the possibility of play in the future, your mind and body are working against each other. You want to live in the big picture and compete in the moment. When things aren't going your way, you have got to embrace adversity, say "So What, Next Pitch!" Let go of the past, and get back to competing in the present moment.

"So What, Next Pitch!" is a verbal key that you can use to help refocus you and your teammates back into the present moment. This key helps you bridge from the past by saying "So What" and returns you where you want to be in the present by saying "Next Pitch."

You cannot just say "So What, Next Pitch!" with your mouth; you have to say it with your body as well. By using your

physical release routine to return to the present, regardless of how you feel about the past play, saying "So What, Next Pitch!" refocuses your mind. You can then actively engage in the most important part of your performance – the next 200 feet.

In life and sport, negative things happen. Adversity is going to strike and there is nothing you can do to stop it. Some tragedies are simply outside of your control. What you cannot do is allow yourself to get caught up in a moment that has already passed. You must constantly move on to the next play. This "So What, Next Pitch!" mentality is emblematic of a peak performer.

 For more on how to develop the So What, Next Pitch! mentality, be sure to visit www.SoWhatNextPitch.com and check out Cain's second book.

REFOCUS SIGN

When I enter the dugouts of top baseball and softball teams, I often hang up a sign at one end of the dugout that says, "REFOCUS." I teach the players that when they recognize their minds starting to wander, they only have to look down the end of the dugout and refocus on the sign. Using the sign as a focal point, gets them back into the next pitch. This is another very simple, yet highly-effective tool to help you get back into the present moment.

THE RECOGNIZE – RELEASE – REFOCUS CYCLE

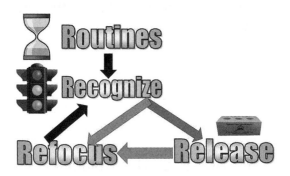

The process of recognize-release-refocus is an important one to master in your pursuit of performance excellence. This process is founded on an internal awareness of your signal lights, especially the ability to recognize when you are out of your green light mentality. Upon recognizing your yellow or red light state of mind, you must make a present moment performance change by performing your release routine in order to refocus for the next play.

This process is conceptually simple and highly effective, yet it is amazing how many athletes neglect this cycle to maximize their performance potential. This is one of the mental conditioning systems that separates the good from the great performers. If you want to perform at a consistently high level of excellence, you must learn how to recognize your signal lights, release frustration from past plays, and refocus on the present moment in competition.

ACTION STEP: When you have adversity and bad calls that go against you, use the verbal for release – refocus which is "So What, Next Pitch!"

EVAN LONGORIA ESPN E:60

Evan Longoria, third baseman for the Tampa Bay Rays was featured in a fantastic video on ESPN E:60. It is one of the best educational videos I have ever seen on mental conditioning and features my mentor Dr. Ken Ravizza. I encourage you to watch this video and pay close attention to the importance of routines for recognizing, releasing and refocusing.

You can find a link to this video by visiting www.MentalConditioningManual.com.

A REALISTIC LOOK AT "THE ZONE"

I do not think you will ever be in green lights for an entire game. If you find yourself in "the zone," with that relaxed intensity and your green lights on steady, then enjoy the ride. It is an experience you may have once; maybe never. Over the careers of the greatest performers on the planet, this kind of "zone" may happen only a handful of times.

Peak performance is not about being in "the zone" all the time and having everything in the game go your way. Realistically, this will likely never happen. Adversity is built into the fabric of sport, making every competition unique, and full of new variables and situations for players to overcome.

Peak performance is about playing your best when you need it the most. It is about compensating and adjusting your performance to the present moment conditions of performance. It is about handling and managing pressure better than the opposition. It is about rolling with the punches until you get the job done. The better your routines and the more systematic your approach, the better your chance to stay in the green lights and perform on the level of excellence.

Great athletes embrace adversity. They welcome it and they starve for it, because they know their ability to overcome adversity is what makes them great.

KNOW YOUR 4R CYCLE

You want to go out and work on your release and refocus routines every day. It may only be for 2-5 minutes, but as part of your in-competition routine, you want to work on your ability to recognize your physical and mental state, release, and refocus on the present.

If you know what your red/yellow lights are and you fail to make a performance change by implementing release and refocus routines to return to your green light mentality, then you are not maximizing your performance potential. You are no better off than your competitor who has not invested the time to read this manual and has not cultivated a deeper understanding of the mental game.

Knowing what to do, but not doing what you know means you are no better off than the person who has no idea what to do. Be a "Do-er," not a "Know-er."

CHAPTER #9 REVIEW

- The ability to recognize your physical, emotional, and mental state within the context of your competitive environment is absolutely necessary.

- Green signal lights – you are giving yourself the best opportunity for performance excellence.

- Yellow signal lights – you are starting to lose the mentality conducive to peak performance.

- Red signal lights – You are totally out of control and it is reflecting in your performance.

- Mastery of performance awareness is developed by understanding your self-talk, physical feelings, and how you deal with common situations during performance.

- A routine-based mental maintenance system keeps you at the peak of the Inverted U of Performance.

- To be consistent over time, you must be able to describe your routines as a process.

- The purpose of your release is to have a physical routine to help you get back in control of yourself and back into your green lights.

- Release your mental bricks.

- All releases should be directed at a consistent focal point.

- Be sure to take a deep breath during your release.

- When you have a mental brick, relieve your mind and "Flush It."

- Refocus on WIN (What's Important Now).

- Develop a "So What, Next Pitch!" mentality to refocus when adversity strikes.

- Use a refocus sign as a focal point.

- Peak performance is not about being in "the zone"; it is about making the necessary adjustments to perform consistently at a level of excellence and to be able to compensate and adjust.

NOTES:

NOTES:

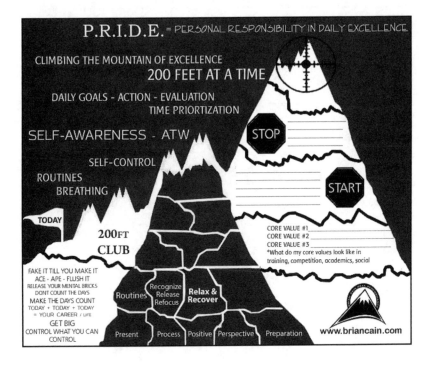

CHAPTER #10

Most coaches and athletes I work with have a hard time relaxing. As a peak performer, you spend a lot of time acting differently than how you feel and forcing yourself to keep on grinding and working to take your performance to the next level. The reason why many coaches and athletes have a hard time relaxing is that a large part of their life is spent making themselves do the things they may not feel like doing but that are instrumental to peak performance. This shows the necessary dedication and resolve to being the best; however, quality time devoted to relaxation and recovery is also necessary to maximize performance potential.

The ability to relax is essential to peak performers, and it is fundamental to developing peace of mind both during and away from performance. When it comes to your ability to relax, you cannot make yourself relax, you must let yourself relax. This performance state seems diametrically opposed to the intense focus demanded for performance excellence and is, therefore, difficult for most athletes to achieve. When you are in a relaxed state, however, your heart rate is lower, your breathing becomes deeper, and this kick starts the body's and brain's recovery and repair process. The more relaxed you are, the quicker you recover from the demands you place on yourself and the quicker you can get back to performance and preparation, as you continue your climb up The Mountain of Excellence.

CAIN'S COACHING POINT: Relaxation is a skill that must be practiced and is a skill that can be developed with proper training, just like the fundamental skills of throwing, running, and jumping.

THE ABILITY TO RELAX IS ALREADY INSIDE OF YOU

Everything you need to relax is already inside you. The world's most powerful tranquilizers already reside within your body. You have the ability to use these tranquilizers to put you to sleep at night, and you can train yourself to tap into one of your body's and mind's most powerful resources throughout the day when you experience stress, pressure, and anxiety. Athletes have reported to me they know that, if they could relax, it would help their performance. So knowing they need to relax is not the problem; the problem is that they often do not know how, because they have never been taught the simple strategy for relaxation.

Let's face the fact that when a coach or teammate says to you, "Hey, Brian, just relax!," it does not help your performance. In reality, it often makes you more tense, because now you know that your teammate or coach has picked up on the fact that you are stressed out and full of anxiety. As a player or coach, instead of telling someone to relax, ask them to take a good deep breath. Taking a deep breath is the single most valuable and effective exercise the athlete must learn to enter a more relaxed state.

THE CALMING OF CAIN

 When I was a college baseball player at The University of Vermont, the part of my game that held me back the most was my inability to relax and keep my mind productively focused in the present moment, one pitch at a time. My mind would get moving so fast that I could not keep it on the one thought that mattered— the execution of that particular pitch. My mind would be thinking about how this was my opportunity to make up for my previous mistakes, to finally show my coaches, teammates, and myself that I was good, that I was worthy of the scholarship I had been given, and that, if I could perform at the level of my expectations, I could get drafted. As you can tell, the gears would begin to move faster and faster until I could hardly breathe, and before I knew it, I was ready to come out of the game before it even started.

In senior year I took a stress management class with the University of Vermont Gymnastics Coach Gary Bruning. Luck for me, it was more of an applied stress management class than a theory-based class. He taught the class how to mentally and physically relax instead of teaching textbook theories of stress management and all the physiological effects of stress. I was very aware of the fact I did not know how to relax, so I embraced the opportunity for self-improvement, as Coach Bruning taught us all how to do.

He had us lay down on the floor and talked us through a deep breathing exercise. I put my hand on my stomach and focused intently on breathing in through my nostrils and out through my mouth, while feeling my stomach rise with the inhalation and lower with the exhalation of each breath. After about 5 minutes of feeling weird just lying there and feeling like I should be doing something else, with my mind racing 100MPH, I finally experienced my mind slowing down and my body and mind relaxing.

I was 22 years old in my senior year of college, and can vividly remember experiencing the ability to relax for the first time in my life. It was a revolutionary mind-body experience, and utterly unfamiliar to me. I could slow my mind down and focus into the present through my newfound ability to relax. I could now also speed up my recovery process simply by focusing on my breathing. To this day, I am grateful that I enrolled in that course and for Coach Bruning's applied method of teaching.

MAXIMIZING OXYGEN IN THE OCTAGON

As a mental conditioning coach, nowhere have I seen relaxation and deep breathing serve a more vital function performance excellence than in the Ultimate Fighting Championship. The world's most combative competitive sport of mixed martial arts is a ballet of violence by nature, and some people may find it too brutal for their liking, but this cannot discredit the impressive mentality it takes to step inside of the Octagon and go to battle. As athletes and coaches, we can learn a lot from what happens mentally inside the Octagon that can assist peak performance in other sports.

In mixed martial arts, it is often the fighter who can relax first and move the fight into his specialty who wins. While the fighters work on bringing the fight to them, some of the greatest coaches in the game can be heard in the corner of their fighters reinforcing the importance of breathing to help their athletes relax. As a coach, the verbal cue for an athlete to take a breath is a reminder of what the athlete must do to calm down and perform at a more relaxed state. The more an athlete practices his breathing exercises to relax and quiet his mind outside of the octagon, the more the brain and body know how to respond when he takes the deep breath inside the octagon. As with everything in peak performance, you must learn to be in control of yourself, physically and mentally, before you can control your performance, and the most crucial practice to gain self-control is deep breathing.

RELAXED INTENSITY

The truly excellent peak performance athletes teach themselves how to perform with a relaxed intensity. These performers become so immersed in their present moment focus while simultaneously being so calm and poised that their competitive concentration appears unbreakable. Nothing can distract them; no adversity fazes them. They are "locked in" and it is as if they are playing on another level. Well, it is, because they ARE on another level; this is performance excellence.

CAIN'S COACHING POINT:
This peak performance state of excellence
is different than "The Zone." Personally,
I believe "The Zone" to be a place of
quiet mind and quiet body where you are
performing at your best. But it is a place
that we waste too much time talking about
and trying to get to. I do not believe you
can recreate "The Zone," but I do believe
that you can get much closer to the state
of peak performance, through mental conditioning of
distraction control, battling and dealing with adversity,
acting differently than you feel, and competing all out,
all the time. I invest my time in coaching how to mentally
persevere, have good bad days, and do not focus on
getting into "The Zone." Remember, if you focus on
developing an excellence process, the result will take
care of itself.

RELAX FOR RESULTS

Many coaches will ask me to teach them the secret to performance when the pressure to produce results is at its highest. They want me to teach their team how to produce when it is a 3-2 count and the bases are loaded in the bottom of the 9th inning. What they fail to understand, however, is that there is no secret key to unlock performance when you need it the most. The best way a player or team can respond to the situation is to relax and trust in his mental and physical conditioning. This gives him the best chance for performance excellence.

So, when coaches ask me this question, they are usually surprised when I lead the team away from their performance arena to a quiet and controlled environment and instruct them in methods of relaxation. The performer must be able to relax in a quiet and controlled environment before they will ever be able to relax in the face of adversity. The deep breath and ability to relax is the most powerful tool in the peak performance toolbox and is critical to unlocking your potential, so you can become "locked in" during performance.

RELAXATION IS A SKILL ANYONE CAN DEVELOP

As with all mental conditioning techniques, relaxation is a skill that can be learned and developed. It is a skill that requires mastering all the material previously covered in this manual. The ability to relax is founded upon a present moment focus on the process along with a perspective of positivity that has been practiced over and over so that it has become routine.

I want you to think of the ability to relax as a skill just like the physical skills you use in your sport. If you can throw a football, throw a baseball, slap a hockey puck, or kick a soccer ball, your ability to execute that skill is because you have trained yourself to perform it. You have practiced and you have conditioned that skill, investing time and effort into improving it. I want you to do the same for the mental conditioning skill of relaxation.

THE 5-4-3-2-1 TECHNIQUE

I want to walk you through a relaxation technique called the 5-4-3-2-1 relaxation technique. By understanding how to breathe properly and practicing the process of a 5-4-3-2-1 relaxation technique until it becomes a routine relaxation procedure, you give yourself the best opportunity to relax under pressure and perform at your best.

CAIN'S COACHING POINT:
I have created a 5-4-3-2-1 relaxation training audio that you can download for free by visiting www.MentalConditioningManual. com/extras. If you are interested in having your own custom relaxation program similar to the ones I do for the athletes I coach one-on-one, contact me at customaudios@ briancain.com and we can discuss creating a custom track for you and/or your team.

Visit www.briancain.com/itunes for your free copy of my 5-4-3-2-1 Relaxation Training Audio track you can use to train your relaxation response.

TWO TYPES OF BREATHING

There are two types of breathing: diaphragmatic breathing and shoulder breathing. Diaphragmatic breathing is deep breathing, using your diaphragm and abdominal muscles. To identify this type of breathing, place your hand upon your stomach and feel your abdominal muscles expand as you inhale, and contract as you exhale. During this deep breathing, air entirely fills your lungs and maximizes oxygen intake. Shoulder breathing, on the other hand, only reaches the top of your lungs. Often referred to as shallow breathing, shoulder breathing is often the result of a performer's inability to relax, resulting in tight muscles which exacerbate this tight breathing. As a performer, you must learn the proper method of deep breathing.

It is also important to know where to breath. For proper relaxation, one should inhale through the nose, because the nose acts as a natural air filter, and exhale out your mouth, giving you a more forceful release. As you inhale, I want you to think about a count of 4-6 and, then as you exhale, I want you to think about a count of 6-8, making your exhalation a little bit longer that your inhalation.

SCRIPT FOR THE 5-4-3-2-1 RELAXATION SESSION

This is a script that you can read to your team to help them practice and develop the skill of relaxation. You will want to read it slowly and in a monotone voice.

The first thing I want you to do is put yourself in a quiet, comfortable environment. I want you to sit up straight in your chair, hands in your lap or on the desk in front of you, feet flat on the floor. I want you to look at a spot on the wall in front of you. I want you to focus on that spot.

Now, let your eyes gently close as you inhale. As you inhale, your shoulders and chest should not move. Focus on breathing steadily and deeply through the nose, pushing out all your abdominal muscles as your diaphragm expands and air fills the bottom of your lungs. Now, exhale through your mouth, as your abdominal muscles and diaphragm contract and the air exits your lungs.

As you continue to focus on your breathing, having a count of 4-6 on the inhalation, 6-8 on the exhalation, I want you to realize that everything you need to do to relax is already inside you. The world's most powerful tranquilizers lay within. The ability to relax is a skill that needs to be acquired. You need to train to relax just like you do for the skills required to play your sport.

I want you to answer the following three questions as you continue to focus on your breathing. Answer these questions in your mind and notice how these answers just pop into your head:

1. What is 3 X 3?

2. What is your middle name?

3. What street did you grow up on?

Notice how easily and effortlessly the answers popped into your mind. The ability to relax is a skill that can be trained, developed, and called upon just as easily as answering those three questions.

We will now go through a short body scan in which I want you to focus your awareness into the body parts that are mentioned.

When I say the number 5, I want you to let your toes, the balls of your feet, arches, heels, your ankles, your Achilles' tendon, your calves, your shins release, relax, and let go.

When I say the number 4, let your knees, your quads, your hamstrings, your gluteus maximus, your groin, your hips, your whole lower body release, relax, and let go, sinking further and further into the chair that you are sitting on.

When I say the number 3, let your lower back, your mid back, your upper back, your abs, your obliques, your ribs, your pectorals, your whole torso release, relax and let go.

What you will find is that the more relaxed you become, the better you might feel; and the better you feel, the more relaxed you will want to become.

When I say the number 2, let your traps, your shoulders, your biceps, your triceps, your forearms, your hands, your fingers; just release, relax, and let go.

When I say the number 1, relax the back of your neck, the back of your head, the top of your head, your forehead, your eyes, your cheeks, your jaw; let your lips gently part and your tongue hang in your mouth, as a complete and total body of relaxation takes over.

What you will realize is that the more relaxed you become, the better you will feel; and the better you feel, the more relaxed you will want to become.

Take another deep breath.

Now, gently open your eyes. Bring yourself back to this moment, right here, right now.

This concludes the 5-4-3-2-1 relaxation session.

CONTROL THE ENVIRONMENT

In order to properly condition your relaxation, you must begin training in a controlled environment. Initial relaxation training should occur in a quiet and controlled environment where you can relax in peace. This enables you to focus on the process of relaxation in that moment, ignoring all other stimuli and emptying the mind of unnecessary thoughts.

Once you have practiced in this quiet environment for weeks, slowly integrate adversity into this controlled environment to simulate a more chaotic or competitive environment. Introduce crowd audio or music in the background of your controlled setting and practice your relaxation response to this adversity by focusing on your breathing. Audio simulates adversities that will become a distraction, if you let it get into your head. Do not let it get in your head. Use your relaxed state of mind to push distractions far away by locking into what you want to focus on, going one breath at a time.

Once you have trained your ability to relax under simulated adversity, in a controlled environment, the next step is to perform your relaxation technique in performance practices, and then pressure-packed scenarios in game-like practices. During these preparation sessions, you will further practice the execution of your relaxation techniques, and eventually this will translate to an execution and relaxation excellence during competitive performances.

CONTROL YOURSELF

As I am sure you have gathered by now, breathing is the foundation for relaxation. Simultaneously, breathing is the basis for emotional state management, a.k.a. self-control. Relaxation conditions self-control by teaching you how to become grounded within the self. Your body and mind become one in the present moment, as you focus on the breathing. The relaxation process is proven to reduce stress levels and alleviate anxiety, giving you control of your emotional state. Good breathing makes all the difference in self-control, and thus, in the achievement of performance excellence.

CONDITIONING RELAXATION RESPONSE

If you have never trained your breathing and you try to relax by taking a deep breath in a pressure situation, the body and the brain will not be conditioned to respond by relaxing. But, if you condition yourself to relax through the routine practice of deep breathing, first in the quiet, controlled environment, and then in more disruptive scenarios, by the time you call upon it in the heat of competition, it will be a skill you have developed and will manifest when you need it.

When you practice the 5-4-3-2-1 technique, you will feel more connected to the present moment, more relaxed, and more in control of yourself. The more you train with the 5-4-3-2-1 technique, the more you focus on your breathing, and the more you do your relaxation training, the more this relaxation preparation is going to help in practices and performances. The goal is for this technique to become so routine that when you take a deep breath to help you relax, your body's going to be conditioned to respond by relaxing. When this occurs, you will know you have a properly conditioned relaxation response.

RELAXATION IN THE RECOVERY PROCESS

For athletes to take their performance to the next level, they must constantly put their bodies and minds in uncomfortable and stressful situations where they are challenged to adapt and evolve. To consistently bring a high level of energy and effort to these situations, athletes must be able to recover outside of the competitive arena.

Relaxation is a tremendous facilitator of recovery. The more relaxed you are, the greater the recovery process, thus assisting your physical and mental climb up The Mountain of Excellence.

RECOVERY PROCESS

As you are probably well aware, there is a physical recovery process after physical performance in which the body goes to work repairing the damage done to muscle tissue. After a weight lifting session, it is this physical recovery process that builds the muscle you desire for performance. Not surprisingly, there is a mental recovery process of releasing performance stress and anxiety that is equally important. In the recovery process, these two forms of recovery often converge, blending similar practices and exercises to maximize both forms of recovery. All athletes should be aware of the significance of recovery on performance and understand that both your physical and mental recoveries are enhanced when in a relaxed state.

 ACTION STEP: If I were to grade my ability to relax on a 1-10 scale, with 10 being the best, I would give myself a -

1 2 3 4 5 6 7 8 9 10

To help me move one number closer to 10, I will do:

_____

_____

_____

_____

THE MAGIC 20-MINUTE WINDOW

Dr. Declan Connolly is a world renowned exercise physiologist, sports nutritionist, and strength and conditioning coach. He is a professor at The University of Vermont and a consultant to the New York Rangers, among other professional teams and Olympic organizations. He also was my college undergraduate advisor at The University of Vermont and, remains to this day, a close personal friend and mentor on the physiological aspects of performance. Dr. Connolly speaks of the importance of the sports nutrition magic 20-minute window.

The magic 20-minute window of sports nutrition indicates that you want to have food in your system, whether it is a protein shake, a peanut butter and jelly sandwich, or even a Snickers® bar, within the 20-minute period after finishing a workout to help speed up the recovery process.

The recovery benefits of getting food in your system within 20 minutes after the completion of a workout will be greater than it would be if you had steak and potatoes 45 minutes to 1 hour after a workout. Physically and mentally, the recovery process is kick-started when you can get these much-needed proteins, carbohydrates, and fats into your system within that window. Developing the discipline to bring food with you for post-performance snacks is important to enhance your recovery process. It is equally important that you force yourself to act on your knowledge of recovery, because many athletes report they do not feel like eating after performance.

DISCIPLINE IS THE KEY

The hardest part about eating inside of the magic 20-minute window after completing a workout is having the discipline to bring food with you to the gym or the field. Establishing a disciplined routine of bringing yourself a simple peanut butter and jelly sandwich on wheat bread, or a piece of fruit, and getting that food in your system within that 20-minute window, will dramatically speed up your recovery process.

 To listen to an interview with Dr. Connolly about fueling to win and sport nutrition, please visit www.MentalConditioningManual.com/extras. or www.briancain.com/itunes and subscribe to Cain's podcast for free

ONE-THIRD OF YOUR LIFE

If you knew you were going to spend one-third of your life performing a sport, you would want to gather all the information you could and educate yourself on how to achieve performance excellence. If you knew you were going to work a specific job for one-third of your life, I bet you would also want to become as knowledgeable and proficient as possible to achieve job performance excellence. So why would sleep, which you will do for approximately one-third of your life, be any different? Unfortunately, you probably know very little about what goes on physiologically when you sleep, so let's get you started with some general knowledge about the importance of sleep for your recovery.

POWER SLEEP

Dr. James Maas is a professor at Cornell University and one of the world's leading authorities and experts on sleep. In his book *Power Sleep,* he breaks down the information you need to know about sleeping and how much you need it to perform at your peak. As a scholar, he has addressed the physiological benefits of sleep and the issue of severe sleep deprivation that plagues most college and high school athletes, resulting in performances that represent less than 80% of their potential.

An individual is considered to be sleep deprived if they sleep four hours or less per night, while eight hours constitutes normal sleep. The National Sleep Foundation's sleep guidelines recommend seven to nine hours for the average adult and Dr. Mass suggests in *Power Sleep,* that you get 9 hours and 15 minutes of sleep a night so that you will receive your five REM (Rapid Eye Movement) cycles thus maximizing the physiologic benefits of your recovery time in sleep. One night of missed sleep will probably do little harm, but the cumulative effect of poor sleep will have a negative impact on your performance.

Sleep is an active physiological process, one in which your body is busy carrying out vital activities, while you are unconscious. While asleep, your body alternates between two forms of sleep: rapid eye movement (REM) and non-REM sleep. This cycle repeats several times throughout the night. The stage of REM sleep provides the brain with the energy to support it during waking hours and is necessary for restoring the mind to function at a level of peak performance. These physiological processes are significant for your psyche, because mental conditioning is most effective when an individual's psychological state is in sync with an optimum physiological state.

10 TIPS FOR SOUND SLEEPING

1. Relax Before Retiring – Take some time for a pre-sleep ritual to break the connection between stress and bedtime. Try listening to the 5-4-3-2-1 relaxation session or listen to relaxation music, do some light stretching or take a hot shower.

2. Watch the Caffeine – Caffeine is the stimulant present in coffee (100-200 mg), soda (50-75 mg), tea (50-75 mg), and various over-the-counter medications. Caffeine should not be consumed at least four to six hours before bedtime.

3. Watch the Alcohol – Although alcohol is a depressant and may help you fall asleep, the subsequent metabolism that clears it from your body when you are sleeping, causes a withdrawal syndrome. This withdrawal causes awakenings and is often associated with nightmares and sweats. To help reduce some of these effects, try drinking one glass of water for every alcoholic beverage consumed. You should stop all liquid consumption at least 2 hours before bedtime so that you are not waking up in the middle of the night to urinate.

4. Exercise at the Right Time – Regular exercise relieves stress and encourages good sleep. However, if a little exercise really gets your blood pumping, it would be wise to avoid working out in the evening or just before bedtime.

5. Cut Down on Noise, Light, and Extreme Temperatures – Try earplugs, a night light, an eye mask, or drape clip. The best temperature for sleep is 65-69 degrees.

6. Eat Right and Sleep Tight – Avoid eating a large meal just before bedtime or going to bed hungry. It is about balance. Also, whenever possible, opt for foods that promote sleep, such as milk, tuna, halibut, artichokes, oats, asparagus, potatoes and bananas.

7. Understanding Jet Lag – Before you cross time zones, try waking up later or earlier to help your body adjust to the time difference. *It takes approximately one day for each hour you fly to adjust to a new time zone.* Many people are affected more severely by West to East travel than East to West. Anticipate that it may take a few days for your body to catch up, and you can speed up that process by easing yourself on the new time zone schedule before you leave.

8. Respect the Purpose of the Bed – Avoid TV, eating, and emotional discussions while in bed. The mind and body associate bedtime activities with being in bed. Do do not let a bad habit keep you awake.

9. Nap Smart – A power nap early in the afternoon can really refresh you. Make it brief; no more than 20 minutes. Sleep too much and you may spend the night staring at the ceiling.

10. Pet Sleepers - Does your pet sleep with you? This, too, may cause arousals from either allergies or their movements in the bed. Thus, Fido and Kitty may be better off on the floor than on your sheets.

Be sure to invest in the best mattress you can afford. How you spend the eight hours a night you invest in bed, will determine how you are able to invest the other 2/3 of your life that day. Invest in yourself. Invest in your rest and recovery.

OLYMPIC SLEEP TRICKS

The USA Olympic organization will often go into the Olympic Village ahead of the games and put in extended-length beds and blackout curtains in the rooms of all its athletes. This is because the organization recognizes how important sleep is to its athletes' peak performance. It wants to give the athletes the best opportunity to bring home the gold and so it invests wisely in sleep.

You probably cannot travel with blackout curtains, but you could get a pair of ear plugs and an eye mask for under $10.00. If you are a high school or college student and you are living in a dorm where people are coming home late at night slamming doors, roommates are making noise, and there is a constant commotion, make the investment in your sleep time. Earplugs will block much of that noise and the eye mask shuts out excess light. Both items will help with your ability to get an excellent night's sleep.

CAIN'S EXPENSIVE EXPERIENCE ON RECOVERY

When I was an athlete, I always thought I was capable of more than was requested of me and that the longer and harder I worked, the better I would become. I was constantly working out and running, doing more than was expected of me. What I failed to realize was the significant difference between working harder versus smarter, and that the more I worked, the more I needed to recover.

I never had a plan for recovery, or a great sleep routine, and I probably slept around 4-6 hours a night in college. As a result, I broke down, physically and mentally, and I was injured all the time. I was the guy who pulled all-nighters, thinking I could cram all my studying into one or two days, and then regurgitate it on exam day. I would either take course exams so jacked up on caffeine that I would crash in the middle of it, or I would walk in and simply not recall any of the information, because I was so tired. If you are a casualty of poor recovery habits, *Power Sleep* goes into the physiological and psychological problems that come with pulling all-nighters.

Again, it was my course with Coach Bruning that turned my life and recovery routines in a productive and progressive direction. In this course, Coach Bruning taught yoga to the class as a source of both physiological and psychological relaxation. Practicing and understanding the benefits of yoga has really helped me become more familiar with my body and my emotional state management. During that course, I improved my flexibility, learned how to breathe and find my center of balance, both physically and mentally. If you have the chance to study yoga, I suggest you do and become more self-aware.

RE-CENTER YOURSELF

Relaxation and recovery are both critical elements within a peak performer's mental conditioning program. Training your relaxation response through deep breathing will help you stay locked into the present moment, think more clearly, and perform more fluidly during competition. Relaxation, outside of the competitive arena, will help you speed up the recovery process, enabling you to return and perform harder and longer (do not forget smarter!) as you take your performance to the next level. Throughout life, it is important to use these relaxation and recovery practices to constantly re-center yourself, because internal balance leads to the performance consistency necessary for all peak performers. As you climb The Mountain of Excellence, remember to pause, take a deep breath, and re-center yourself. This will keep you climbing at your most productive pace.

CHAPTER #10 REVIEW

- We all possess the ability to relax.

- Aim to perform with a relaxed intensity.

- Relaxation is the secret to results-under-pressure.

- Relaxation is a skill one must develop like any other physical skill.

- Diaphragmatic breathing is superior to shoulder breathing.

- Practice the 5-4-3-2-1 technique to build a relaxation response.

- Begin training your relaxation response in a controlled environment and progress under simulated adversity.

- Emotional state management is all about self-control and breathing.

- Relaxation is instrumental to recovery process.

- Invest in your sleep.

- Relaxation before bed facilitates productive sleep, benefiting physiological and psychological recovery.

- Mental conditioning is most effective when an individual's psychological state is reflective of an optimum physiological state.

- Internal balance leads to the performance consistency necessary for all peak performers.

- You cannot make yourself relax, you must let yourself relax.

NOTES:

NOTES:

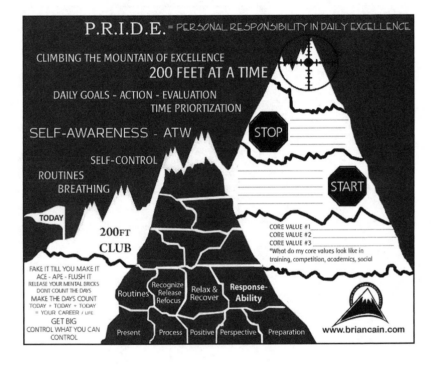

The most powerful ten-word sentence in the English language consists of only seven short two-letter words. That sentence is: *If it is to be, it is up to me.* This encapsulates response-ability.

Response-ability is taking ownership of your past, commanding your present, and taking charge of your future. It is being accountable for your perspective and controlling how you respond to adversity. Too many people are negatively affected by outside influences they cannot control. They respond by becoming a victim of outside factors, rather than responding to adversity by holding themselves responsible for their actions.

In this chapter, the importance of response-ability will be made clear. You will learn how response-ability makes a difference in performance and how to begin disciplining your mind to respond to events in order to produce productive outcomes. The utility within response-ability must be mastered for peak performance; your journey up The Mountain of Excellence will depend on it.

MAN FREEZES TO DEATH - LACK OF RESPONSE-ABILITY

In the February 1978 issue of *Success Unlimited*, psychologist Dr. Dudley Calvert tells the story of a railway employee in Russia who accidentally locked himself in a refrigerator car. Inside the car, he could not unlock the door, nor could he attract the attention of those outside. Unable to escape, he resigned himself to his fate. As he felt his body becoming numb, he documented his story and his approaching death in sentences scribbled on the wall of the car.

"I am becoming colder now," he wrote. "Still colder, now. I can hardly write…" and, finally, "these may be my last words." And they were.

When the car was opened upon arrival at its destination, other railway employees found him dead. Yet, the temperature of the car was only 56 DEGREES! The freezing apparatus had been out of order in the car. There was no physical reason for his death. There was plenty of air – he hadn't suffocated. What happened was he gave away his personal power and defeated himself by not responding appropriately to the challenges in front of him. He let the power of his mind negatively affect his reality. Remember, perspective is reality and you are response-able for choosing any attitude and any perspective you want in any given situation. His own lack of response-ability led to his demise, a victim of his own delusion.

MAN OVERCOMES HELL ON EARTH – RESPONSE-ABILITY

In *Man's Search for Meaning*, Viktor Frankl talks about his unfathomable experience and survival of the Nazi concentration camps in World War II. Frankl, a psychologist, knew he was response-able for his survival in his hell-on-earth conditions. He chose to search for something of value and meaning every day of his struggle.

Living in the concentration camp, Frankl discovered the Nazis could take away his family, his freedom, his food, and health, but they could not take away the last of the human freedoms: one's ability to choose his/her own perspective. Frankl realized that his ability to determine how he responded to his environment was psychological and that his human spirit was still free. With this in mind, he found daily existential meaning and purpose in aiding other prisoners by sharing the little food he did have and offering comforting words.

Unlike our man in the boxcar who went down the path of negativity, Frankl chose a path of positive empowerment. Both men had response-ability. If Frankl could find meaning in and survive the horrific experience of the concentration camps, and a man can freeze to death in a non-freezing box car, imagine what your response-ability can do for you. Imagine what you can endure. Can you survive the perceived challenges of your everyday life and maintain a positive attitude? Absolutely. To be a peak performer, a sense of response-ability is a must.

EVENT + RESPONSE = OUTCOME

There is a simple math equation that I want you to learn and, more importantly, implement.

E [Event] + R [Response] = O [Outcome]

In life, it is not what happens to you, it is how you handle what happens to you. It is your ability to respond (response-ability) that is going to determine your outcome when adversity is thrown your way.

As a human being, YOU have the ability to respond to an event in the manner you deem appropriate. The response is your choice. Humans have the unique ability to socialize their innate responses to events with the three steps of performance change – awareness, strategy, and implementation. We have previously discussed this process, and it provides an essential foundation for full comprehension of E+R=O.

We often do not have much control over the Events in our life, but we do control our Responses. This is an empowering notion, because once you realize that you control half the equation, you recognize that you control half the outcome. If a negative event occurs and you keep a positive present moment focus, with a big picture mentality, and a "Compared to what?" perspective as your response, then you will determine the outcome.

This is the process of mental conditioning that you prepare for through establishing mental routines. The practice of mental conditioning will teach you how to be responsible by accepting the Events, formulating Responses, and, therefore, perceiving the Outcomes. We are all capable of using this process to our benefit in life because we all have the ability to control our responses.

THE HUMAN PAUSE

As was briefly mentioned, humans have the unique ability to become internally aware of their responses to external stimuli. The famous psychological study known as the Pavlov's Dog Experiments represents groundbreaking research investigating conditioned and unconditioned responses to unconditioned and conditioned stimuli. Without going into all the details of classical (Pavlovian) conditioning, the takeaway relevant to mental conditioning is when there is a stimulus, there is a response.

Humans are no different, except for our ability to become aware of our responses. This recognition of how we respond is vital to mental conditioning, because we can train ourselves to pause in between the stimulus and our response. Once we are aware of our innate responses to certain stimuli, we have the power to control and change them. Most people are unaware of this unique human ability, and these are the people we say have poor self-control.

Start becoming aware of how you respond to certain stimuli. To gain awareness and challenge yourself to catch that pause in between the event and your reaction, reflect on how you react to particular events. Those trained in discipline and response-ability face adverse stimuli with poise. They control their pause by taking a deep breath, and responding in a manner conducive to the attainment of excellence. Developing control over that pause is what separates those who stay in control under pressure and those who crack.

Remember it this way: When the dog of adversity threatens with his dangerous jaws, control yourself with your human pause.

EMOTION CLOUDS REALITY

In the heat of competition, it is easy for your mind to become clouded by adversity. When officials make poor calls, the opposition seems to be catching lucky breaks, or you are just not performing to your full potential on that day, it is easy to let your emotions get the best of your performance. As an athlete in pursuit of excellence, do not let your emotions cloud the reality of performance.

When you take emotion out of the picture, you tend to respond much more clearly. What does emotion do? Emotion clouds reality. In my work, I see frustrated people fire off at officials, coaches, players, and athletic directors, and often approach often trivial situations as if they were life or death, not sport. Most times after the outburst, there's regret that emotions overpowered sensible response-ability.

It is important to use the mental conditioning skills we've discussed in this manual to maintain response-ability. This comes back to self-control – recognizing what is within your control and emotionally letting go of everything else. Rely on the "Ps" of peak performance as the conscience that reminds you of your ability to respond with excellence rather than emotion.

THE RULES OF RESPONSE-ABILITY

The greatest coach I have ever had, my mentor at Cal State Fullerton, and an icon in the field of sport psychology, Dr. Ken Ravizza introduced me to his three rules of mental conditioning that I believe truly reflect the significance of response-ability. I believe a peak performer must understand these three rules of response-ability to give himself the personal power to reach the summit of The Mountain of Excellence.

1. Before you can control your performance, you must be in control of yourself.

2. You have very little control of what goes on around you, but you have total control over how you choose to respond to it.

3. What you are aware of you can control; what you are unaware of will control you.

Staying in control of yourself and recognizing what you can and cannot control will allow you to mentally stay in a calm, centered, and grounded place. Staying in control of yourself in the face of adversity is a skill set that must be repetitively practiced for its proper development and will allow you to perform in pressure situations. Understanding what you can and cannot control and choosing to focus on what you can control, while letting go of what you cannot, gives you the personal power to focus your time, energy and attention to achieve excellence. The first step to self-control is having an awareness of what is going on around you and, more importantly, what is going on inside of you. Ultimately, the development of self-awareness will place the power of response-ability in your head.

CAIN'S COACHING POINT: Early on in the manual, you learned the importance of forcing yourself to act differently than how you feel, shouldering that personal response-ability, and choosing to act appropriately regardless of the situation. How have you been doing at acting differently than how you feel? Where in your life can you act different than how you feel, choosing your response-ability, and giving yourself a better chance for success?

ACTION STEP: Where in my life can I demonstrate better self-control?

1) _____

2) _____

3) _____

PRAYER, PRIMAL, & PERFECT

In his book *Heads Up Baseball,* Dr. Ken Ravizza points out that when athletes get emotionally out of control, it usually manifests through their performance in three general ways. They become a Prayer, Primal, or Perfect performer, all of which lead to a decreased level of performance.

PRAYER – When you become the prayer player, you look to some higher power to help you perform. You resign to faith in fate and simply hope for the stars to align and present you with the desired result.

PRIMAL – When you become a primal player, you resort back to the days of the caveman. You begin to perform in a desperate and erratic manner that often leads you out of control and emotionally frustrated and the desired result remains elusive.

PERFECT – When you become the perfect player, you attempt to make everything perfect. You strive for performance perfection and little mistakes prevent you from appreciating the beautiful imperfection of the game. As we have discussed, performance oriented around perfection is a sure path to failure because nothing is perfect. Remember, performance is not about perfection, it is about progress.

As a performer, you DO NOT want to fall under any of these categories.

The defining question at the highest levels of competition is not who has the most physical talent, because, physical talent is, for the most part, similar at the highest levels of performance. Instead, the question is who is able to bring his mental talents to the table on a consistent basis and has the ability to respond appropriately under the pressures of adversity.

As a performer, you want to move away from Prayer, Primal and Perfect and into PREPARED and PRESENT. Mental preparation will assist you in the development of appropriate response-ability, giving yourself the best opportunity for performance excellence.

TRAIN YOUR RESPONSE-ABILITY

Peak performance is contingent on personal response-ability in daily excellence. It is all about being accountable for your perspective and controlling your response to the adverse events that will inevitably occur during performance. Use the equation $E + R = O$ as a reminder that you control half of the equation and the outcome is a result of your perspective. When you train your response-ability, you place the power in your head.

All peak performers learn to take ownership of their past, command the present, and take charge of their future. Once you instill these values within your performance, you will gain the self-control necessary for performance excellence. Do not become a victim to events. Become a champion by developing the ability to respond appropriately to adversity. We all have the ability to respond appropriately, and the material throughout this manual gives you the resources to do just that. The Mountain of Excellence calls out to many performers, but the ones who reach the peak are those who have the response-ability to master the journey and overcome the adversity The Mountain of Excellence will put in your path.

CHAPTER #11 REVIEW

- **If it is to be, it is up to me.**

- **Response-ability is taking ownership of your past, commanding your present, and taking charge of your future.**

- **Event + Response = Outcome**

- **When the dog of adversity threatens with his dangerous jaws, control yourself with your human pause.**

- **Emotion clouds reality; learn to control it.**

- **Develop self-control by learning the three rules of response-ability.**

- **Prayer, Primal, and Perfect are all undesirable states of performance mentality.**

NOTES:

www.briancain.com

NOTES:

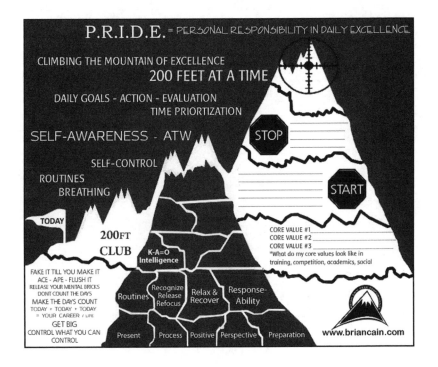

CHAPTER #12

INTELLIGENCE – K-A=O

In 1658, English philosopher Thomas Hobbes wrote "scientia potential est" – translated as "knowledge is power." Many of my teachers referred to this phrase in school as motivation to learn. Well, what they didn't teach me about this phrase, was that it was only half of the story.

Knowledge is empowering, but what is truly powerful is utilization of that knowledge. You can have all the knowledge in the word, but if you do not Get Off Your Anatomy (GOYA) and put it to use, then you are no better off than the person who does not have that knowledge.

If you know what to do but you do not do what you know, you are no better off than the person who does not know what to do.

If you have read this far and have not been highlighting, performing the exercises, or making the effort to practice some of the skills explained in this manual, do yourself a favor and STOP reading. YOU ARE WASTING YOUR TIME! If you are not taking the time to usefully implement your knowledge, you are not acting intelligently. You are not maximizing your performance potential. You may conceptually know more than your opposition, but if you do not invest in mental conditioning as part of your preparation, you are really no better off than the person who does not know that mental conditioning exists.

On the other hand, if you have been underlining, taking notes, performing the exercises, and making the effort to transform the knowledge within this manual into concentrated action, I applaud you. You truly aspire to be a peak performer and represent the select few who are committed to performance excellence.

A simple equation provides some clarity between the relationship of knowledge and action.

K (Knowledge) – A (Action) = 0 (Nothing)

You can know everything but if you fail to take action, you are never going to accomplish anything.

DEFINING INTELLIGENCE

Intelligence is the ability to acquire and apply knowledge and skills. In reading this manual, you have acquired knowledge about the mental game. Conceptually, this material is matter of fact and as straight forward as it gets.

Mental conditioning is simple, but it is simultaneously powerful. Knowledge of mental conditioning is, as aforementioned, empowering, but its true power resonates in the individual's ability to apply acquired knowledge by cultivating skills. These skills harness the power of knowledge through the process of an individual taking action, giving the individual the final ability to exercise these skills through performance. Performance excellence is only achieved through the successful repetition of this process to improve one's skills. It is this process of action that illustrates the excellent performance of knowledge – intelligence.

CAIN'S COACHING POINT:
Athletes, one of the things you say that rubs your coaches the wrong way is "I Know." When you make a mistake and a coach corrects you, please refrain from saying "I know." Remember, it does not matter what you know as much as it matters what you DO! Actions speak louder than words. I have worked with athletes who say, "Cain, we went over this last year. You got any new stuff?" As you climb The Mountain of Excellence, you are constantly evolving and you are a totally different person today than you were one year ago. The fundamentals are the fundamentals, because they are fundamental. Do not be fooled into thinking it is all about the next best thing, because the best thing is a fundamental approach that is refined and reshaped to be done more effectively and efficiently then it was in the past. Your journey up The Mountain of Excellence may consist of walking the same path on more than one occasion. However, each time you walk that path, you are different, the path becomes slightly different, and it is a completely new journey to dominate.

THE EXPERIENCE FACTOR

There are two types of experience that you gather over your career and both reflect performance intelligence. Expensive and inexpensive are two examples of experiences you are constantly gathering to help you learn, grow, and take your performance to the next level. Expensive experience comes from making your own mistakes and errors of judgment to learn life's many lessons. This is considered learning the hard way, as you try to figure out everything on your own. On the other hand, inexpensive experience is when you learn life's lessons from the expensive experience of others; learning from their past mistakes and successes. The knowledge of response-ability we learned from our friend in the boxcar and from Viktor Frankl are examples of inexpensive experience. Their hardships and those of the people you know are all examples of lessons we can learn from others, so that when we are faced with similar adversity we can use this knowledge intelligently to be more response-able and give ourselves the best chance for success.

Some experiences must be expensive, but a great deal of stress and frustration is preventable. There is much to learn through the expensive experiences of others, such as historical figures, coaches, teachers or parents. Learning from the expensive experience of others is the epitome of performance intelligence. The knowledge gained from others and implemented appropriately to maximize performance is what every peak performer aims to successfully accomplish. Proper advice and guidance should be welcome, because the ascent up your Mountain of Excellence is a timely and difficult journey. Utilizing the resources at your disposal will assist your climb and is paramount to peak performance.

Much of this manual is a collection of expensive experience, organized and presented so that you may learn from prior pursuits of excellence. Realize that you are not the first person to have pursued your goals or embarked on a similar journey up The Mountain of Excellence. If you are truly committed to your performance, you must start to accumulate inexpensive experience. When you learn from others you speed up your learning curve and increase your chances for success by intelligently approaching the adversity you will endure as you climb The Mountain of Excellence.

THE MILLION DOLLAR QUESTION

One of the best ways for you to gain inexpensive experience is to ask those who have gone on the journey up the same or similar mountain you are climbing the million dollar question:

What do you know now that you wish you had known when you were on your journey up The Mountain of Excellence that would have helped your performance?

Asking this question can help you to uncover inexpensive experience that is invaluable to your personal education and will help you on your journey. Someone's expensive experience will help you to perform more intelligently because you will be more mentally equipped for the challenges that lie ahead.

I encourage you to ask your elders the million dollar question. If you are a freshman athlete, ask your successful senior teammates for advice. If you are a senior, ask your successful alumni. Ask your coaches or trainers for their advice. Ask parents and members of your family. Asking this question separates those who simply enjoy the game from those who desire performance excellence. Ask the question, and learn from others' experiences.

ACTION STEP: Now that you know the difference between expensive and inexpensive experience, what I challenge you to do today is talk with someone more successful than you about inexpensive experience in different areas.

If you are on a college or high school team, what is some academic inexpensive experience you can gain from upper classman that could speed up your learning curve? What athletic experience can you learn from your teammates?

Ask one of your coaches about something that they know now that they wish they knew when they were in your position? Coaches are ALWAYS willing to share their expensive experience in the hope that it may become inexpensive experience for their athletes.

As a selfless peak performer, share your experiences with those embarking on a journey you have already done or have already started. If you are presently in college, go back and share your experiences with your high school program to assist its learning curve. Many people aspire to reach the summit of The Mountain of Excellence, so be a mountain guide for those at base camp by sharing your experiences.

SHOW YOUR INTELLIGENCE

There is no power in knowledge. The power is in action. You want to surround yourself with people who are educated, so seek out great mentors, and learn from their expensive experience.

This mission is a short one, because the importance of intelligence is straightforward. Understand that you must learn from other people, you need to be coachable, and accept constructive criticism in order to turn that knowledge into intelligent action. If you are willing to accept constructive criticism, people will give it to you straight and not sugar coat what you really need to hear. This helps speed up your learning curve and propels you to peak performance.

When you can surround yourself with knowledgeable teachers and mentors, you will absorb their knowledge. As you climb The Mountain of Excellence, taking this action dramatically increases your chances of reaching the summit.

 For my Top Ten Pieces of Inexpensive Experience Visit www.MentalConditioningManual.com/extras.

CHAPTER #12 REVIEW

- Intelligence is the ability to acquire and apply knowledge and skills.

- K – A = 0 [Knowledge minus Action means Nothing]

- GOYA (Get Off Your Anatomy)

- Expensive experience is when you make your own mistakes and errors of judgment to learn lessons.

- Inexpensive experience is learning from past mistakes and successes of others.

- The million dollar question to ask your elders is "What do you know now that you wish you had known then?"

- The process of action that illustrates the excellent performance of knowledge is intelligence.

NOTES:

NOTES:

_____

_____

_____

_____

_____

_____

_____

_____

_____

_____

_____

_____

_____

_____

_____

_____

_____

_____

_____

_____

_____

_____

_____

_____

_____

_____

_____

_____

_____

NOTES:

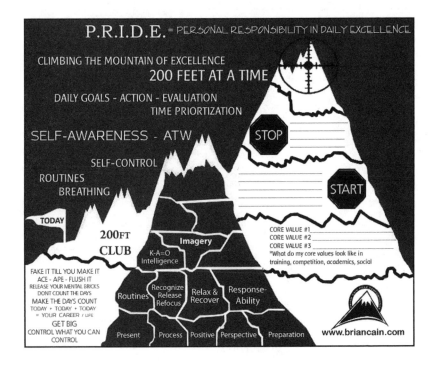

CHAPTER #13

At this moment, imagine standing on the highest level in the center of a podium. This podium is situated in an enormous stadium, and as you look around you suddenly realize the air is being filled by thunderous applause reverberating around the arena. The stadium is full of people and they are standing out of their seats. As you stand atop the podium, taking in the sights and the sounds, you realize this standing ovation is for you.

It is a medal ceremony at the Olympic Games and you are the gold medalist in your sport. You turn to your right and on a slightly lower podium stands the silver medalist, who is beaming from ear to ear as he nods in acknowledgement and then waves to the crowd. As you turn to your left, you see the bronze medalist standing on an even lower podium, waving enthusiastically to what you could only assume to be family in the stands.

A voice over the loud speaker announces the beginning of the medal ceremony for your sport, followed by the announcement of the bronze medalist. You watch from atop the podium as the bronze medalist, and then the silver medalist receive their medals, until it is finally your turn.

Your name and title are announced and the crowd responds with another great wave of applause, and you return the acknowledgement with a smile. An Olympic organization official approaches you along side the medals carrier with only the gold medal resting on the tray. You lean forward, as is custom, and the gold medal is placed over your head.

As you stand there and the gold medal settles against your chest, a final and total comprehension of your achievement washes over you. This is it. In this moment, you have reached the mountain top.

As you stand on the highest level of the podium, you stand at the pinnacle of your sport. With utmost satisfaction, you know you have given your best when you needed it the most, and that your performance has been simply superior to the competition. As you stand tall and proud listening to your country's national anthem, your PRIDE, that personal responsibility in daily excellence, your making all of your todays count, and not counting them over all those years of training, has culminated in gold. The game has rewarded that PRIDE. Now, all the world watches and recognizes you as the ultimate peak performer, the epitome of performance excellence.

This imaginary scenario is just your introduction to mental imagery. Let's make it a reality.

HEAD REHEARSAL

One of the most underutilized mental conditioning skills today is mental imagery. Mental imagery, often referred to as visualization, is the process of creating mental experiences that resemble actual physical experiences. This process is similar to the stimulation of the imagination when you read an excerpt in the second-person narrative, such as the introduction to this chapter. The difference is that the script is not on a piece of paper in front of you; it is all in your head.

In mental conditioning, mental imagery is used to enhance performance preparation. It is a technique employed to exercise the mind by mentally creating the environment of performance competition and mentally performing the competitive tasks required in your sport. Mentally, you rehearse how you want to feel and how you want to perform, imagining the integration of your physical conditioning and your mental conditioning within your mind.

THE MIND-BODY CONNECTION

Mental imagery has the potential to make a real impact in your performance. Whether you vividly imagine or you physically execute your performance, the brain processes those two experiences with similar psychoneuromuscular pathways. Mental imagery is physiologically creating neural patterns in your brain in the same manner as the performance of a physical action. Essentially, if you are lying in bed at night before competition and you practice mental imagery, you are imprinting the blueprint of your performance in your mind, further embedding those pathways and enhancing your capacity to achieve performance excellence.

CAIN'S COACHING POINT:
Before you get carried away, however, let's get one thing clear: mental imagery is not a substitute for physical preparation. This is not some shortcut or fast-track to peak performance. Putting in the physical time is priceless. What the mental conditioning technique of mental imagery does, is enhance your physical abilities by deepening those psychoneuromuscular pathways in your brain. Mental imagery is utilized to maximize the efficiency and effectiveness of your physical preparation.

YOU ARE "THE ARCHITECT"

In order to emphasize how an individual practices mental imagery, I've drawn a parallel to it and a concept from the Warner Brothers' blockbuster movie *Inception*. In the film, a complex plot revolves around dreams and characters' movements in and out of the dream world. There are particular characters in the movie called "architects," who build infinitely detailed dream worlds that mirror reality. This movie is one of the ultimate mindbenders in cinema, and if you haven't seen it, I apologize for using this particular analogy. However, this concept of "architects" is exactly what you want to emulate in your process of mental imagery.

When you perform the mental conditioning technique of mental imagery, you create a mental world. You construct in your mind a psychological replica of your sport's competitive arena (gymnasium, stadium, etc.), placing you and your opponent within that arena, performing your sport. When you perform mental imagery you want to build in the sense of sight, the sense of sound, and the sense of touch. You want to mentally experience the appearance of your competitive arena and the face[s] of your opponent[s]. You want to experience the energy in the arena. If you are playing away from home, imagine the away crowd heckling you from the sidelines. You want to experience yourself making the plays that will make the difference at competition's end. Some athletes even integrate the familiar smells of their competitive arena into their mental imagery. The more details you construct as the architect, the greater you enhance the effectiveness of the mental imagery experience.

PHYSIOLOGICAL BENEFITS FROM PSYCHOLOGICAL STIMULUS

If you are still a little skeptical about mental imagery, then I want to give you a little taste of the mind-body connection. I want you to experience the physiological response to the psychological stimulus of mental imagery. Before telling you to just go off and practice mental imagery, I am going to walk you through a scenario in the next section.

Whenever you perform mental imagery, recall and practice the techniques of relaxation you will learn in Chapter 17. So sit back and become relaxed. Go through the process of relaxation and practice your deep breathing as you read the passage.

I am going to walk you through a scenario where you go into your kitchen, reach into your refrigerator, pull out a lemon, cut lemon wedges, and take a bite out of one of those lemon wedges. Read slowly and imagine the scenario in all its detail. Practice utilizing all your senses in this passage, because you want to make this scenario feel as real as possible in your mind.

THE LEMON EXPERIMENT

Start by taking 3 good breaths on a 4-6 count on your inhalation and on a 6-8 count on exhalation. Breathe nice and deep; in through your nose, and release out through your mouth.

Now, imagine walking into your kitchen at home. Feel what the floor feels like on your bare feet.

You are now standing in front of your refrigerator. See your refrigerator in front of you in all its detail. Now, extend your hand outward, reaching for the refrigerator door, and clasp its door handle.

As you open that refrigerator door, notice a nice big, bright yellow lemon on the top shelf.

Reach for it and grab it. As you hold it in the palm of your hand, see the skin and feel the coolness and texture of that lemon as you feel its weight in your hand.

Now, put that lemon on the counter, take a knife lying there, and use it to cut the lemon in half the long way. See the juice and the body of that lemon as the knife slices through. Smell the slightly sour scent released into the air.

Take half of the cut lemon and cut it again, so that you have two equal wedges. See and feel the sting of the lemon juice on your wet fingertips. Breathe in that scent swelling in the air.

Now, gently place your fingers, wet with lemon juice, on either side of a lemon wedge and lift it off the counter. Bring it up to your mouth and close your lips around the wedge before sinking your teeth along the lemon rind and squeezing the lemon juice into your mouth. Feel the lemon juice squirt onto the back of your tongue and the back of your mouth. Feel that sensation at the back of your teeth as you press your tongue against them to get all the lemon juice.

Remove the lemon and place the deflated wedge back on the counter.

A TASTE OF THE IMAGE

Did you have a bit of a puckering sensation? Did your mouth salivate at the thought of the lemon taste? Could you smell that lemon or feel the sour juice sting your taste buds? Just thinking about the process of eating lemon made me salivate while I wrote this passage.

If you did receive any of those sensations as you read the passage, then you have now consciously experienced a physiological response – the body responding to a psychological stimulus. This is a simple first-hand experience that emphasizes the shared psychoneuromuscular pathways of the brain. Remember this experience and try to simulate the realness of eating the lemon in your mental imagery.

If you did not experience a physiological response, then you probably read the passage too fast and didn't immerse yourself in this psychological scenario… or maybe you just do not eat enough lemons! But seriously, in order to properly utilize mental imagery, you MUST use the techniques of relaxation you will learn in Chapter 17. You must become absolutely immersed in the present moment mental rehearsal you are performing, releasing all mental bricks and deflecting all distractions.

MENTAL REHABILITATION

One of the best ways to maintain your edge while injured and recovering from injury is to use mental imagery. If you cannot practice your sport, there is no reason why you cannot mentally prepare yourself for physical performance. Often called mental reps, players use mental imagery to imagine themselves doing all of the physical skills they would be doing that day in practice. This mental rehabilitation really provides a huge psychological advantage in the physical rehabilitation process by keeping the performance specific psychoneuromuscular pathways in your brain active.

When a player is finally physically ready to perform, those psychoneuromuscular pathways are just as game-ready. By maintaining active psychoneuromuscular pathways, there is no dusting off the mental cobwebs and there is no regaining your mental edge. Your brain has been mentally preparing during the whole process of rehab and is fit and ready for performance. By knowing how to practice mental imagery, there is absolutely no reason to lose your mental edge.

MENTAL IMAGERY PAYS BIG DIVIDENDS

When he first broke into the league in 2005, NFL quarterback Matt Cassel was the backup for Tom Brady and the New England Patriots. In 2008, after a Week 1 season-ending injury to reigning NFL MVP Tom Brady, Cassel was thrust into the starting role on the Patriots' offense. These were big shoes to fill, but Cassel was surprisingly cool about the transition.

There was a great deal of fascination surrounding Cassel, due to his inexperience in the starting role. In fact, Cassel had not started at quarterback in a football game since he was in high school and, according to ESPN research, Cassel is the only known quarterback to start in the NFL without having been a starter in college. Cassel had attended the University of Southern California (USC) and had been the backup quarterback to Heisman trophy winners Carson Palmer (2002) and Matt Leinart (2004).

What made Cassel so quietly confident was his preparation, particularly his use of mental conditioning. In a *Sports Illustrated* article, Cassel discussed how he would wear a helmet on the sideline with the Patriots and would hear the play being called in from the offensive coordinator. He would then call the play cadence out loud on the side line, as if he was in the huddle.

When people asked him, "Why do you do that?" Cassel would respond, "I call that play out loud and then I visualize what the play would be. I, then open my eyes, watch the field and see if the image I had in my mind is what happens on the field. I play the game one play at a time mentally so that, when I get thrown in the game as a back-up quarterback, I am not surprised, I am not caught off guard, I am always right in the mix of that game mentally."

His mental imagery performance paid off as Cassel led the New England Patriots to an 11-5 season. Despite not making the post-season with their winning record, due to a highly-competitive division, Cassel's season, based on his leadership and performance, was a success. At season's end, the Patriots used their franchise tag on him, extending him a one-year contract worth over $14 million, the largest one-year contract for an offensive player in NFL history. Cassel ended up leaving New England in an off-season trade to the Kansas City Chiefs, where he went on to sign a six-year, $62.7 million dollar contract. As you can see from the experience of Matt Cassel, mental imagery pays big dividends.

MENTAL PERFORMANCE BEFORE PHYSICAL PERFORMANCE

Athletes across the spectrum of sport use some form of

mental imagery prior to performance. In Saul Miller's book *Hockey Tough*, Paul Kariya, an NHL all-star from the University of Maine, said, "I score 50 goals a day in my mind before I ever leave the hotel for the arena." This is the mentality of a peak performer; mental rehearsal before physical performance.

Many baseball players I work with will have four at-bats per game. Before the next game, they will replay those four at-bats in their mind, always imagining the outcome they desire – quality contact with the ball. Those players will imagine their at-bats another four times before they go to bed. The performance of mental imagery is giving those players a competitive advantage over their competitors. They are able to take the four at-bats they expect in the game and turn them into twelve by the end of each night, thus getting three times the number of at-bats as their competition, and facing the pitcher three more times than the pitcher faces them. This builds experience and confidence in their preparation for performance. By mentally rehearsing quality at-bats, these players give themselves a greater opportunity to realize this outcome during their physical performance.

VIDEO ENHANCEMENT

I cannot emphasize enough that, when you are doing mental imagery, you want to make the experience as game-like as possible. You want to utilize all of your mental capacity to make the images appear vivid and clear. A technique sometimes used to assist mental imagery is watching video of yourself performing before you do mental imagery. Witnessing yourself play on tape is not only good for understanding how you perform, but also can aid the practice of mental imagery because using past performances to conjure images helps provide details to mentally rehearse future performances.

I encourage the athletes I work with to create a personal highlight video that they watch before they do mental imagery. This enables them to relive their best performances and then re-imagine their feelings in those scenarios through mental imagery.

PRACTICING ADVERSITY

A great way to utilize the benefits of mental imagery is to create a list of situations in your sport that make you uncomfortable and represent some form of adversity. Once you have made this list, use it as a checklist and use mental imagery to perform under each adverse scenario and execute exactly the way you want to in performance. This is similar to the favorite physical practice of children acting out a last-second scenario, where their team is down one and they hit the game-winning shot as time expires. Both practices deal with adverse situations and both imagine a desired outcome.

IMAGINE YOUR EXCELLENCE

Mental imagery is one of most basic and fundamental of all mental conditioning strategies; however, it is widely underused. Remember that actions speak louder than words. You now have a greater understanding of the power of mental imagery, so it is up to you to DO mental imagery in order to increase your performance and prepare more effectively for your journey up The Mountain of Excellence.

CHAPTER #13 REVIEW

- Mental imagery is the process of creating mental experiences that resemble physical experience.

- Mental performance physiologically creates neural patterns in your brain in the same manner as the performance of physical action.

- As a mental architect, you want to build experiences of all the senses within your mental performance.

- Mental imagery enhances psychoneuromuscular pathways to assist physical rehabilitation.

- Practice mental performance before beginning physical competition.

- Watching videos of your best performances benefits your mental imagery by giving you a positive visual.

- Practice handling adversity in mental imagery as you do during preparation.

 Please visit www.MentalConditioningManual.com/extras to download your free Mental Imagery training audio tracks for your sports performance.

NOTES:

NOTES:

NOTES:

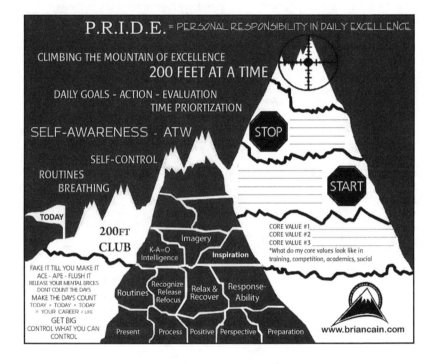

CHAPTER #14

INSPIRATION & MOTIVATION

I was in Dallas, Texas at a fair and on a stage was a big, muscular strongman. He was performing some amazing feats of strength – ripping phonebooks in half and bending crowbars with his hands – to the applause of his audience.

In one of his acts, he pulled out a lemon and squeezed all the juice out of that lemon and said, "Ladies and gentlemen, I am a strongman. I've squeezed all the juice out of this lemon. I will give $1,000 to anyone who can come up and extract one more drop."

In response, two giant Dallas-Cowboy-like guys went on stage to give it a try. The first guy grabbed the lemon and gave it a good, hard squeeze. No drop. The crowd laughed in amusement as he stepped back to let his friend give the lemon a squeeze. The crowd went silent and watched the second guy give the lemon a squeeze, contorting his face in grimaced concentration. He suddenly released his grip with a gasp for air, but still, not one drop of lemon juice.

The crowd laughed and applauded as the two men exited the stage. The strongman was left on stage holding his arms in the air with the lemon in his hand, when he saw an old lady, who looked to be in her seventies, walking up the stairs onto the stage.

The strongman said, "Ma'am, for the sake of time, can we move on? You are not going to squeeze any juice out of it. I mean, c'mon. The guys who just tried couldn't do it and they looked like professional football players."

"Sir, just give me a chance," the old lady said politely. "I have a big reason WHY."

"Okay. Here you go. One chance," said the strongman, who handed her the lemon as the crowd cheered in support.

The old lady took the lemon within her hands and began to squeeze. Her face became contorted. Her jaw set. Her veins began popping out of her forehead. Her glasses fell off her face. Her entire body shook back and forth from her intense struggle with the lemon as she squeezed it with all her might.

BOOM!! Out popped one drop of lemon juice.

The audience erupted in applause! The sounds of clapping, whistles and cheers rang throughout the fair. The strongman was blown away as he was compelled to show the audience the plate on which the drop of lemon juice had fallen. The old lady stood there onstage with her hands on her knees as she collected her breath. It was a scene to behold.

Then, the strongman walked over with a check he had just written out for $1,000 and handed it to the lady, as he said, "Ma'am, you have got to tell us. I've never had anyone squeeze an extra drop of juice out of that lemon. How did you do it?"

She replied, "Sir, I have to tell you. I am 74 years old. I just lost my husband. I've got three grandchildren that we're raising and I just lost my job. I needed that money."

The old lady was inspired. *She was motivated. She had a reason WHY she needed to squeeze that juice out of the lemon and with a big enough reason why, you will always find a way how.* The reason why is the fuel that burns the fire of inspiration and motivation inside of you.

So what is your "why"? Why do you do what you do? Why are you reading this right now? What do you want to accomplish in your life, this season, this week, today? What is your process for making those dreams a reality?

Most people think inspiration and motivation are things that you can do once in a while by reading a book, watching a movie, or hearing a motivational speaker. Most people think that is all it takes for you to stay motivated. The reality is, that could not be further from the truth. Although those experiences may spark a flame, in order to fan the flame, to make it burn with a passion, you must have a BIG reason why.

MOTIVATION IS A DAILY DECISION

Imagine only brushing your teeth once a week. I hope, for everyone's sake, that you are disgusted by the thought of brushing your teeth only once a week. Your teeth would become yellow, feel hairy, and your teeth would develop cavities and/or rot, in addition, nobody would want to hold a conversation with you because your breath would blow them away. My point is that you cannot brush your teeth once a week and expect them to look or feel good.

Inspiration and motivation work the same way as dental hygiene, except it is not for your oral health, but your mental performance health. You should mentally absorb some form of inspiration daily to motivate you in your preparation and performance. Do not read something inspiring once a week. Do not motivate yourself or your team once or even a couple times a week. Inspiration and motivation must be performed every single day.

ADVERTISE TO YOURSELF

Have you ever wondered why companies are willing to pay three million dollars for a thirty-second commercial during the Super Bowl? The common response to this question is that tens of millions of people watch the Super Bowl. This is true, but the real reason is that advertising works. Ads create lasting images within the mind, so that when

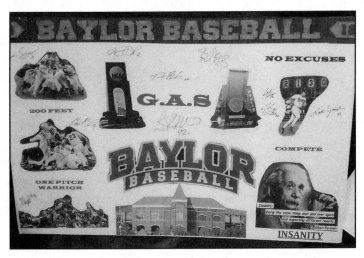

people go out to consume products, those products from the advertisements jump to the front of their minds.

The same tactics of advertising apply to inspiring peak performance. Advertising to yourself will enhance your preparation and competition by inspiring your performance. Similar to any marketing consultant, before creating sporadic marketing pitches you must know what it is you are trying to advertise and the most effective methods for marketing that product. With mental conditioning, the product is the mindset of a peak performer. Advertising to yourself through various strategies will help you to create the peak performance mentality you desire.

KEVIN YOUNG – OLYMPIC ADVERTISING

The current world record holder in the 400-meter hurdles, with a time of 46.78 seconds, is the 1992 Summer Olympic gold medalist Kevin Young. When Young got to the Olympic Village in Barcelona, he advertised his Olympic goal to himself by writing it down, everywhere. When asked about his preparation in an interview after his world record performance, Young responded by saying, "My goal this year was to run 46.89. I wrote that everywhere in my room, even here up at the village. I took a pencil and wrote it all on the wall. I integrated it into a lot of things I do at home. I just got into the habit of writing the number around, everywhere I go."

Young used the power of self-advertising his goals by putting his goal in writing, where he could see it often for motivation. As an aspiring peak performer, you too should advertise your goals to yourself by putting them everywhere you can see them. If you truly desire something, you should be able to visualize it as you go through your day at every turn. Self-advertising helps you to focus on what you want not what you are trying to avoid.

ACTION STEP: What goals can you write out and post around your room?

1) _____

2) _____

3) _____

SIGNS OF SUCCESS

An excellent habit to develop is collecting inspirational phrases, pictures, and images to create "signs of success" to hang around your living space. This provides you with visuals for motivation that you will see on a daily basis. When you see these signs of success every day, it becomes a part of your everyday thought process. After a few days or a week seeing a particular sign, your goal will be to commit this sign of success to memory and, more importantly, to have it effectively motivating you to action.

I self-advertise signs of success by hanging photos, quotes, and other images all around my home and office. I have pictures of athletes and coaches who inspire me, quotes that motivate me to continuously check my perspective, and mental conditioning statements, such as "Do not count the days, make the days count," as reminders of the importance of today. Whenever I need them, these inspirational advertisements catch my eye and keep me inspired and motivated in my journey up The Mountain of Excellence.

TCU BASEBALL SIGNS OF SUCCESS

Texas Christian University head baseball coach, Jim Schlossnagle, is one of the best college coaches in the country. He has a series of signs that hang in their dug-out and help create the mindset he wants his team to maintain on a daily basis. The signs of success are simple ways to advertise the peak performance mentality and mental conditioning principles you want to adopt in sport and life.

MAKE YOUR OWN SIGNS OF SUCCESS

Draw from the material and information you have acquired from this manual and make your own signs of success. By creating your own signs of success, you put your knowledge of peak performance to use and enhance the process of mentally conditioning excellence.

 ACTION STEP: Based on the content within this manual, what are three captions for signs of success that you will hang in your room to stay inspired?

1) _____

2) _____

3) _____

EXAMPLES OF SELF-ADVERTISEMENT

Now that you know the importance of the signs of success and have created captions for you self, let me share with you what other athletes have reported hanging in their rooms as self-advertisements. Remember, at all levels of competition, you are never too good to stay inspired.

1. A vision board collage of all your goals and what you want to accomplish.

2. A picture of your national or state championship arena where that event will be held.

3. A poster of Muhammad Ali or other athletes who inspire the mentality that you want to develop.

4. A poster of The Miracle On Ice or other great moments in sport that motivate you to do the work it takes so that you too may experience a similar great moment

5. An inspirational quote from your favorite piece of literature.

BATHROOM MIRROR – DRY ERASE MARKER

Another great technique you can use to stay inspired is to write your goals on your bathroom mirror with a dry erase marker. Whenever you enter the bathroom, you will see your goals and be reminded of the mindset you want to develop to become a peak performer. Essentially, your mirror becomes a goal-oriented sign of success.

I have worked with professional mixed martial arts fighters who arrive in Vegas at their hotel, and the first thing they do upon entering their room is take out a dry erase marker and write their mental game reminders on their mirror. This sets the tone for their peak performance mentality, because whenever they enter the bathroom, they are reminded of their desired mindset and to focus on that mindset and process for performance excellence.

GOAL CARDS CARRIED ALL THE TIME

Another strategy you can use is to carry a goal card in your wallet. Carrying a goal card will make you 35 percent more likely to make those goals come to fruition, because you have the constant reinforcement whenever you open your wallet. Whenever you do open your wallet, take a look at that goal card and mentally check in with how you are moving forward to achieve that goal. This form of self-advertising will go wherever you go.

ATHLETIC TAPE & WRIST BAND ADVERTISING

During preparation or in competition, a great method of self-advertising is to write inspirational messages on athletic tape or wrist clothing. Wrist tape and wrist bands are effective places for self-advertising because you constantly see the messages in front of yourself. Many baseball players will write their goals inside their hat so when they take it off, they are reminded of what they must work on or are trying to accomplish.

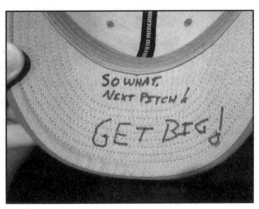

VISION BOARDS

One of the best motivational exercises you can do as an individual and as a team to help with inspiration and motivation is to create a vision board. A vision board is simply a collage of your goals and what you desire to accomplish. I strongly encourage you to create a vision board for yourself, and if you are on a team, I highly recommend you create one together as a team-building and team-focusing exercise. When you create a visual image of what it is you want to accomplish, you increase your chances of accomplishing that goal by 35 percent.

You will never outperform your self-image. Making a vision board of images will inspire you to accomplish your goals. Place it where you will see it every day. This will keep your goals in the front of your mind and motivate you to achieve them. I personally started using vision boards in 2007 and annually revisit my own vision board the first week in July. Below is a picture of my personal vision board.

As you can see on my vision board above, I want to speak in every state in the country. The ones that are white are the ones that I have not had a chance to speak… YET. I want to help teams win national championships (accomplished in 2012 – Alabama Softball). I want to spend more time fishing and hiking in the mountains of Vermont. I want to read at least one book every month. I want to be a better listener. I want to keep my weight under 200 pounds (198lbs at present). I want to have better balance in my life between work and relaxation, and I want to live the core values of being positive, disciplined, progressive, and committed to others. I also wanted to be a #1 Best Selling Author, which has been accomplished with my first book *Toilets, Bricks, Fish Hooks And PRIDE.*

I keep my vision board with me in my binder and I look at it multiple times each week. I have a copy of my vision board on my desk at home, and on my desk at the office. The vision board serves as a reminder for me to constantly ask myself: Is what I am working on right now helping me get to where I want to go? The vision board is great for helping create the awareness you need to constantly check in on your progress towards achieving your goals and to refocus you on what you want to accomplish.

TEAM VISION BOARD

The creation of a team vision board is a simple and powerful team-building activity. Similar to the perspective poster, the best way to make a team vision board is to start off with each person creating his own and presenting it to the team. By doing this with your team, you improve your chances of accomplishing your goals.

When everyone is done presenting his individual vision board each teammate should select one item that would go on the team vision board. He should explain why he selected the item he did and why it is important to the program. You can use words, photos, drawings – really anything and everything – to help you create that visual representation and reminder of your team goals.

WORK TO MAKE "IT" WORK

Here's the significant difference between peak performers and the rest of humanity: peak performers understand that you must work to make "it" work. Whatever that "it" is, it is all about investing time and energy into a process of development that will make you excellent at what you do, and thus, bring you success. The vision board process has worked for me, it has worked for Jack Canfield, author of *Chicken Soup for the Soul,* and it has worked for thousands of other people.

If you are an unenthusiastic pessimistic cynic, colloquially referred to as a "Debbie Downer" or a negaholic, and you believe that, "This mental conditioning stuff is bogus. Thinking about things does not help you do it. It is never actually going to improve my performance," then, well, you are right. Since you have made it this far in the manual, it is clear you are not one of these people. My hope is that, based on all the previous missions, you can see it is quite apparent this imaginary skeptic obviously has zero knowledge about how peak performance and mental conditioning apply to the journey of excellence.

What real life skeptics do not understand is that you have to work to make it work. The reason mental conditioning exercises will not work for them is a result of their refusal to try and make it work. It is not rocket science that if you do not attempt to make something work, of course it will not. It is the same logic as the old saying, "You miss 100 percent of the shots you do not take." You must believe in the benefits of mental conditioning for your performance to improve, and there are real, tangible pay-offs.

The use of signs of success and vision boards will help you stay focused on your goals and will help you to get motivated and stay inspired to DO THE WORK that it takes to be successful.

CAIN'S COACHING POINT:
If you noticed anyone on your team who has openly dismissed mental conditioning and stopped reading this manual, reflect on how his attitude and actions affect the team. If his mentality is adversely affecting team chemistry, I'd suggest confronting that teammate or making your coach aware of the situation as an expression of genuine concern for the well-being of the team throughout the season. Sometimes these moments can make all the difference in an athlete's career, or even the person's life, because someone took the time and cared enough to step up, maybe more than that person cares about himself.

MOTIVATIONAL MOTION PICTURES

The use of motivational videos, inspirational movies, and highlight reels, are another tremendous tool for peak performers. Similar to the video enhancement in mental imagery, there is no debating that watching some form of motivational motion picture or video before a practice or a game will inspire your performance on that day.

Watching a motivational video clip every morning as part of your morning routine also provides great reinforcement for the kind of person you want to be today. Regardless of how you feel when you wake up, the video clips you watch will get you fired up to dominate that day and do the work necessary to advance further up The Mountain of Excellence.

 ACTION STEP: I challenge you to make your own personal highlight video. You can use footage of you or of others on YouTube to inspire your performance to keep climbing to your summit on The Mountain of Excellence.

 To see some of the personal highlight videos I watch, visit www.MentalConditioningManual.com/extras

INSPIRE YOUR INTELLIGENCE

Whether you read a chapter in this manual, watch an inspirational movie clip, or any number of the various methods for inspirational motivation, you must build motivation into your daily routine to become inspired to take action. You will have more success spending 3-5 minutes a day getting inspired and motivated than you will if you spend one hour, once a week. This will set the tone of your mentality and encourage you to dominate the day. Remember, if you get inspired a little a lot, you will have more success than if you get inspired a lot a little.

By the end of using this manual, you will possess the information necessary to transform yourself into a peak performing athlete. It is, thus, imperative that you motivate yourself to master the mental game in your daily preparation and performance ACTION, not just develop a masterful comprehension of the material in this manual. Remember, intelligence is acting on the knowledge you have acquired. Use the knowledge from within this chapter to inspire your climb up to the summit of The Mountain of Excellence.

CHAPTER #14 REVIEW

- Have a big reason "why" and you will always find a way how.

- Make yourself inspired daily by reviewing motivational material.

- Advertise your goals to yourself.

- Make signs of success for motivation.

- Write daily goals on your mirror and make longer term goal cards.

- Self-advertise during performance by writing on athletic tape.

- Create vision boards for performance goals.

- Work to make your goals a reality.

- Watch motivational video clips for inspiration.

- If you get inspired a little a lot, you will have more success than if you get inspired a lot a little.

NOTES:

www.briancain.com

NOTES:

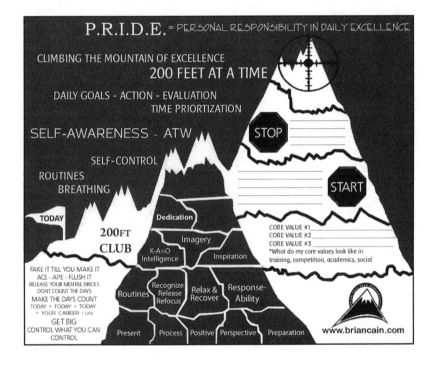

CHAPTER #15

DEDICATION & COMMITMENT

It is one thing to become inspired to accomplish a goal by surrounding yourself with motivational images, quotes, and materials that give you a big enough reason why, but it is another thing altogether to take that inspiration and put it into action. Once you know your why and you have the inspirational tools in place to help you stay motivated to conquer The Mountain of Excellence today, it takes dedication to continue the grueling ascent and commitment to make the necessary progress on a consistent basis. The previous chapter reviewed methods to instill inspiration and keep you motivated, increasing the likelihood of taking action. The importance of actually dedicating yourself to inspired peak performance is addressed here.

DEDICATION

Dedication is the unwavering ability to commit oneself to a particular course of action, and to preserve an attitude of perseverance despite all adversity and hardship. To be dedicated to a purpose can, at times, be challenging and all-consuming, but the pursuit of excellence is not for the faint of heart and meek of mind. A peak performer must display a steadfast dedication to personal development and a resolute commitment to improving their performance competency. The Mountain of Excellence is a treacherous climb, and only those who dedicate their heart and their soul to conquering the mountain will reach the summit.

DEVELOPING DEDICATION

The development of dedication takes a sense of purpose and constant discipline. For the individual athlete, dedication must be fueled by an internal flame and must be fanned with a purpose and big reason why. As an individual performer, you must take pride in the personal satisfaction your sport brings you and you must devote yourself to defeating limiting beliefs that challenge the human psyche and soul.

As a team athlete, one of the first steps in the dedication process is the ability to develop an attitude of gratitude, putting "we" over "me." If you are going to be dedicated to the team, you must be willing to put the success of the team ahead of your own success. When you make a commitment to a group of others, the team synergy allows you to go further than you could on your own.

As an athlete, you have probably experienced being on a workout program by yourself and only being able to reach a certain level of intensity. When you make the commitment to work out with a partner or a teammate, however, you are able to push each other and take the intensity to another level. If you lift in the morning, it is harder to sleep in and skip a workout when you have a workout buddy. Your commitment to your partner keeps you dedicated to the process of physical improvement. This is why I encourage you to have an accountability partner who keeps you dedicated to your mental conditioning and pushes you towards performance excellence. It is always easier to let down yourself than it is to let other people down. Use this principle to your advantage and make a commitment to someone else.

PUBLIC DECLARATION

When you identify what it is to which you are committing, make the decision to surround yourself with people who are dedicated to a similar goal. True dedication starts the day that you make that declaration known to others who can become your support team and hold you accountable for reaching your goals. When you make the commitment to share your goals with others and establish accountability partners to help you stay on task, you are asking for others to make a personal investment in you. When they ask you to be similarly accountable for them, you can return the favor. The establishment of this mutual accountability is essential, because it is easier to let yourself down than it is to let someone else down. Public declaration of your goals and establishing accountability partners helps you stay committed to your journey up The Mountain of Excellence and ensures that you will not be alone in your travels.

It is always easier to quit on yourself than it is to quit other people. You are only able to achieve more if you have the total effort of all team members. How you get there is by everyone committing to each other, by verbalizing your goals, by making your goals public, and then by creating the synergistic, supportive, and positive environment with everybody working together to make it happen.

WHAT IS "TEAM"

A team is any group of people who organize in a cooperative effort driven by a shared purpose to achieve a common goal. It is a collective of individuals who come together and sacrifice individual glory and place the success of the whole group first and foremost by encouraging and demanding excellence from one another. A true team is a family; a band of brothers and/or sisters who discover each other on a similar journey and realize they not only make one another better, they make the journey worthwhile. *In your quest in the pursuit of excellence, creating your team is vital to your ultimate success.*

TEAM HOYT

Dick and Rick Hoyt are a father and son team that competes in Ironman Triathlons, events in which they swim together for 2.4 miles, bike 112 miles, followed by running a marathon of 26.2 miles – without a break. Most Ironman events have a time limit of 17 hours. Imagine the dedication, commitment and training it takes to summit that mountain of effort?

I have run two marathons and have the utmost respect for those doing one after a 2.4 mile swim and a 112 mile bike ride. What is even more impressive about this team is that Dick, Rick's father, actually pulls Rick in a boat for the 2.4 mile swim, pedals his bike with Rick sitting on the front of the bike for the whole 112 miles, and then pushes him in a wheelchair for the full 26.2 mile marathon.

Rick was born a spastic quadriplegic with cerebral palsy as a result of oxygen deprivation to his brain at the time of his birth. The doctors initially told Dick to forget about his son and put him in an institution, but, Dick and his wife decided to raise him like any other child. In the spring of 1977, Rick told his father he wanted to compete in a 5-mile charity run for a paralyzed teenager in order to let them know that life goes on. Responding to this call to action, Dick agreed to push Rick the 5 miles in the wheelchair.

The team completed the race next to last, and that night Rick told his father, "Dad, when I am running, it feels like I am not handicapped." Both avid sports fans, this statement inspired Dick to get Rick participating in more running events.

Since competing in their first race, Dick and Rick have competed in over 1,000 races, including marathons, duathlons, and triathlons, six of which were Ironman competitions. The pair has become known internationally as Team Hoyt, gaining fans everywhere they go and inspiring millions. Team Hoyt represents the epitome of dedication and commitment to family, team, and the pursuit of excellence. The Hoyt's story is one of defeating the naysayers and their journey together is living proof that with the right dedication and commitment any goal is conquerable.

TEAM ACRONYMS

Here are two acronyms for the word "team" that exemplify its spirit.

TEAM: Total Effort of All Members

TEAM: Together Everyone Achieves More

These two acronyms symbolize what it means to be a team. The first embodies the dedication required to achieve collective pursuits and common goals, while the second acronym typifies why teams are so critical to accomplishing that which is often individually impossible. For these reasons, I encourage you to surround yourself in your endeavors with a team dedicated to you, each other, and the achievement of your goals.

TEAM LANGUAGE

If you are on a team, a benefit of going through a mental conditioning program together is the common language you develop. Teaching a common performance language to a program is an effective method to speed up the learning process of the athletes. It will help improve teammate communication around the mental aspects of performance and to help build the collective mindset necessary for unified peak performance. You are never truly alone on your journey up the mountain, so utilize your team to help you get there.

DO YOUR DEDICATION

Dedication is paramount to performing at a level of excellence. You can say you are dedicated and you can say you will commit to your core values and team goals, but what REALLY matters is your actions. Do not bother with talking the talk; peak performance is about walking the walk. Express your dedication to your goals and your teammates every single day, because you are responsible for holding each other accountable to pursuing the summit of The Mountain of Excellence.

CHAPTER #15 REVIEW

- Dedication is the unwavering ability to commit oneself to a particular course of action, and to preserve an attitude of perseverance despite all adversity and hardship.

- Dedication takes a sense of purpose and constant discipline.

- You must be devoted to yourself and devoted to the team.

- True dedication begins when you make a public declaration.

- Accountability partners help you stay dedicated and accountable for your performances.

- Team is a group of people who organize in a cooperative effort and is driven by a shared sense of purpose to achieve a common goal.

- TEAM = (Total Effort of All Members) & (Together Everyone Achieves More).

- Do not talk the talk of peak performance, walk the walk.

NOTES:

NOTES:

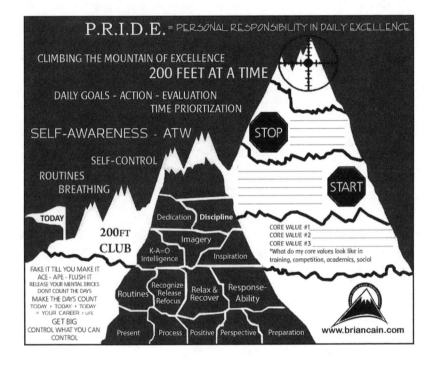

CHAPTER #16

With self-discipline anything is possible. Without it, nothing is possible. Self-discipline may be the biggest separating factor between the performers who make it to the summit of The Mountain of Excellence and those who fall short. If you have the self-discipline to invest your time appropriately, to follow proper sports health principles, and to perform with the same tenacity in preparation as in competition, all on a daily basis, then you are well on your way to reach the summit.

Once you have acquired the knowledge necessary for performance excellence in any field, the challenge is to master yourself and establish the self-discipline to perform on a consistent basis. For peak performance, obtaining the knowledge necessary to perform at a level of excellence is the easy part, while the difficult part is acting on that knowledge to show performance intelligence. We reviewed this concept in Chapter 11, but intelligent performance is founded on the establishment of self-discipline to the process. It is the self-disciplined intelligent execution of performance knowledge that elevates you throughout your climb up The Mountain of Excellence.

CONFUSION ABOUT DISCIPLINE

Many people can be confused about the value and importance of discipline because they think of the word in a negative context. At one high school where I was working as the Athletic Director, we had an Attendance and Discipline office. It should have been called the Attendance and Lack of Discipline Office, because the only time students got called down was then they did something stupid – lacked mental, physical, or verbal self-discipline. This goes to show that people often have a negative association with the word discipline. Discipline in peak performance, however, is not only something that happens to you when you break a rule, it is something that you possess as a high achiever.

DEFINING DISCIPLINE

How do we define discipline? In peak performance, we define discipline as the possession of trained control of oneself and one's conduct for personal improvement and performance progress. In mental conditioning preparation, the concept often becomes simplified to doing what you should do regardless of how you feel. *Disciplined athletes and disciplined people do not feel much different than those who lack discipline, they simply have learned to act different than how they feel.* Discipline, however, is how to keep yourself on course as you ascend The Mountain of Excellence and is one of the most important fundamental skills you should develop if you want to be a peak performer.

WAYS TO DEVELOP SELF-DISCIPLINE

Despite being the cornerstone of implementing mental conditioning, discipline itself must be developed the same as any component of mental conditioning. Self-discipline is a skill that can be cultivated as if it were a fundamental skill of your sport and, actually, it is. You acquire proficiency over the fundamentals through the process of repetitive training, and self-discipline is improved through the same process of repetition through daily practice.

DEVOTE YOUR TIME

Success in any field is usually more time-consuming that it is difficult. It takes tremendous self-discipline to invest the amount of time it takes to be successful. Malcom Gladwell discusses in his book *Outliers,* the "10,000 Hour Rule." claiming that the key to success in any field is the investment of 10,000 hours into practice. Athletes like Tiger Woods, musicians like Joshua Bell, and tycoons of technology like Bill Gates have invested tremendous amounts of time into their craft. Although I will agree to disagree with Gladwell and others about the rule of 10,000 hours, there is no debating, that to reach the summit of the highest mountains, you must possess the skill of self-discipline.

THREE DAILY DISCIPLINES

University of West Virginia Head Baseball Coach Randy Mazy is one of the top coaches in all of college baseball. At the beginning of the season, he asks his players to perform three tasks, without fail, every single day. Whether they want to, already do, or do not feel like doing them is irrelevant. The three tasks he has them do every day are:

1. Make their bed.

2. Shave their face.

3. Wear their seatbelt.

As you can see, these are not difficult tasks and do not require a whole lot of effort. All it takes to complete these tasks is for athletes to wake up five minutes earlier to make their bed and shave when they get out of the shower. Most of them, hopefully, already always wear seatbelts when they drive, so all they need to do whenever they hop in a car is make sure to reach over their shoulder and buckle up. Then why exactly is Coach Mazy asking this of his players?

The purpose of performing these three tasks on a daily basis is merely to establish disciplined routines in the lives of Coach Mazy's athletes. In laying this foundation, Coach Mazy forces players to become consciously aware of what discipline is and how it is practiced. Then, when they need to establish a particular routine, physical or mental, for their baseball performance, his players have a reference point for developing self-discipline and acting different than how they feel.

ESTABLISH YOUR OWN THREE DAILY DISCIPLINES

The ability to develop the habit of self-discipline is imperative in peak performance. That is why I ask you to thoughtfully reflect upon areas where you could improve your self-discipline. After you have thought about it, list three tasks you can perform to improve your self-discipline. Your discipline goals could be focused on nutrition, sleep, hygiene, academics, time efficiency, etc.

 ACTION STEP: What are three daily tasks you can perform to improve your self-discipline?

DISCIPLINE GOAL 1)_____

_____

DISCIPLINE GOAL 2)_____

_____

DISCIPLINE GOAL 3)

PRACTICING MY PREACH

One thing I have always struggled with is nutritional discipline. When I became an athletic director, I found myself in front of the computer more than the weights or the treadmill and my weight swelled to about 230lbs. As a 6'1" guy, I wanted to get down to under 200lbs. I felt like garbage, ate garbage, and I looked like garbage. Then a friend of mine called me out on my health and asked me, "How can you go around the country and talk about discipline and excellence when you are about 30lbs overweight? You know, you are probably losing credibility every time someone sees you in person." I was stopped in my tracks and forced to do some soul searching. This was exactly what I needed to hear and, at that point, I knew I needed to start practicing what I preached on self-discipline.

That evening, I dedicated myself to improving my all-around health and losing those unwanted 30lbs. I established daily goals that took concerted effort and self-discipline to accomplish. I sat down and made the time to create a workout calendar, as well as, got in contact with some friends I knew who worked out. I told them about my new goal to lose weight and get in physical shape so that they could hold me accountable to that goal. Between my new workout partners and my workout calendar, I was motivated to establish the discipline necessary to get myself in physical shape.

Once I did this, I knew the hardest part would be nutritional discipline. So, I made the time to develop my own nutritional plan where I ate on the odd hours of the day from 7:00am to 7:00pm. This kept me disciplined about "when" I ate, but I knew I also had to develop self-discipline about "what" I ate. On this daily schedule, I calculated my calorie intake, along with how many calories I was burning from my workouts. I knew that roughly 3500 calories was a pound, so I knew that if I was burning 3500 calories more than I was taking in per week, or burning 500 calories more than I was taking in per day, I would lose roughly a pound a week.

My plan consisted of eating the same thing at the same time every day. There was zero room for error. I made all of my meals on Sunday, because that was the day of the week when I had the time to cook at home. I allowed myself a cheat day on Saturday eating anything I wanted so that I would not burn out following an all-or-nothing nutritional plan. I had the map I needed to keep me disciplined on my journey, and when I would get frustrated during the week, I would remind myself that if I could stay disciplined until Saturday, I could enjoy that cheeseburger and fries on my cheat day. Knowing I had the cheat day built into my schedule gave me the light at the end of the tunnel each week and the process of following the plan changed from a lifetime of diet to just a few more days. The process worked beautifully for me and I know it will work for you.

WHAT MADE THE DIFFERENCE FOR ME

The implementation of my new health programs made all the difference in my personal health and lifestyle. Because I had a specific program in place, I was able to discipline myself to adhere to the system and achieve the results I was looking for. Surprisingly, it was actually much easier and more enjoyable than I had anticipated. Having the

BRIAN M. CAIN MS, CAA
NUTRITIONAL PLAN 6/23/08 - 6/30/08

(Meal #) 0:00	Foods	PRO (g)	FAT (g)	CARB (g)	H20 (oz)	Other	Cal	Total Cal
Meal 1 7:00 am	1 Cup Yoghurt 1 Cup Blueberries 1 Cup Strawberries 1 Cup Kashi - Go Lean Crunch	12.9 1 1 9	3.8 .5 .5 3	17.3 22 12 37				
Meal 2 9:00 am	Golden Delicious Apple Banana	0 2.5	0 0	17 52			65 200	265
Meal 3 11:00 am	Turkey Sandwich 2 Slices Wheat Bread	41 3.1	7 1	0 13.5			240 75	315
Meal 4 1:00 pm	Baby Carrots (10) Sugar Snap Peas (10) Celery Sticks (1 Cup)	0 0.7	0 .2	1.3 3			65 200	265
Meal 5 3:00 pm	Peanut Butter & Honey Sandwich 2 tbsp Peanut Butter 1 Slice Wheat Bread						190 120	310
Meal 6 5:00 pm	Labrada Carb Watchers Lean Body Shake 10 oz Water	40	4.5	12	40		250	250
Meal 7 7:00 pm	Dinner with Family Not to Exceed 500 Cal Salad Ground Turkey Brown Rice Cheese							500
EXTRAS	Water 64 oz None After 7:00pm				64			
TOTALS	DISCIPLINE GRADE FOR DAYS 1-10 Mon ( ), Tue ( ), Wed ( ) Thurs ( ) Fri ( ), Sat ( ), Sun ( )							2200

Brian Cain Peak Performance, LLC is proud to announce a new partnership with Labrada Nutrition, the World's most trusted name in sports and performance nutrition.

If you are reading this page in *The Mental Conditioning Manual,* you are a person committed to mental and physical conditioning as well as personal excellence. Because of that, Labrada Nutrition is offering you a special VIP partnership pricing on their nutritional supplements so that you can be fully fueled for your journey to the summit of The Mountain of Excellence.

 Visit www.MentalConditioningManual.com/extras or www.BrianCain.com to sign up for your special VIP partnership pricing and order instructions.

schedule motivated me to stay disciplined and I ended up not using my cheat day on counterproductive foods and, instead, continued making healthier choices. I was seeing the results of the discipline in following my plan, both physically in my appearance and mentally in my focus and energy levels. Success breeds success and the small wins I experienced gave me the confidence to stick with the plan, and eventually I reached the summit of that mountain and could begin to climb another.

Now that I am healthier and more disciplined about my health, I realize how important it was that my friend called me out on my physical condition. Upon reflection, that friend was the first person who cared enough about me to be completely honest to my face. It was just the reality check I needed. This is the importance of accountability partners. You should always be able to rely on someone to tell you those inconvenient truths to keep you honest.

PROGRAMS ARE PRICELESS

What I had been missing from my life up to this point had been the plan of action to establish self-discipline over my physical condition. This leads to an important life lesson: If you set out to accomplish a goal but have no plan, you are setting yourself up for failure. It would be like taking a trip to New York City, and without a map of the city, trying to find a specific restaurant without knowing the address. You have a chance, but not a good one.

If you research those who are most successful, you will find that they all possess great self-discipline and adhere to personal programs to achieve excellence. Programs and self-discipline go hand-in-hand for the pursuit of performance excellence. They force you to establish a plan of action and hold you accountable to it. Along with accountability partners, the establishment of a program gives you the best opportunity to establish the self-discipline you need to achieve performance excellence.

DISCIPLINE YOURSELF

This mental conditioning manual is designed to provide the training program and strategies you need to take action and design your own programs to scale your desired Mountains of Excellence. My high school football coach John T. Allen always told the team one of his favorite quotes from Coach John Wooden, "Discipline yourself so other people do not have to." I challenge you to heed the advice of these two great coaches. Start working on your self-discipline by establishing a few things you will do on a daily basis, by having accountability partners, and by implementing processes and routines that you will follow on a daily basis to propel your journey to the summit or The Mountain of Excellence.

CHAPTER #16 REVIEW

- Discipline is the possession of trained control of oneself and one's conduct for personal improvement and performance progress.

- Do what you should do regardless of how you feel.

- Self-discipline is a fundamental life skill.

- Discipline takes a concerted effort and devotion of time.

- Begin cultivating discipline by establishing three daily disciplines.

- Programs are priceless because self-discipline is a process.

- "Discipline yourself so other people do not have to."
  – Coach John Wooden

- Act differently than how you feel.

NOTES:

NOTES:

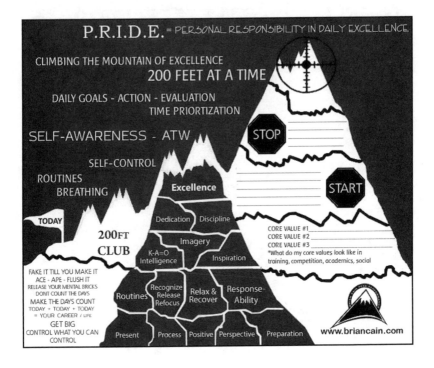

CHAPTER #17

Excellence is being at your best when it means the most – every single day.

This concept rules supreme in peak performance, transcending and penetrating all other aspects of mental conditioning. It is assuming personal responsibility in your daily pursuit of excellence that will make you a champion, because consistency of effort wins. Excellence is about the cultivation of superior mental strength through the process of establishing the proper routines, positive self-talk and mentality in preparation for inevitable confrontations with adversity.

After all the mental conditioning material we have covered in this manual, you should be both informed and well on your way to achieving your goal of performance excellence. Throughout the PRIDE Program, we have outlined the fundamental principles of mental conditioning and discussed how to adapt these principles and apply them on your journey to the summit of The Mountain of Excellence. This chapter explains the purpose of necessary devotion to excellence within performance.

EXCELLENCE IS A LIFESTYLE

Excellence is a lifestyle, not an event. Truly excellent individuals recognize that excellence is not something you do once in a while; you must strive to be excellent all the time. That is twenty-four hours a day, seven days a week, and three hundred sixty-five days a year.

THREE DOORS & THE LAW OF AVERAGE

You have three doors you can choose to open. You can open the door called WIN, you can open the door called LOSE, or you can open the door called EXCELLENCE. The pursuit of excellence is about more than winning; performance excellence transcends it. Excellence is a lifestyle; winning is an event that takes place therein.

Remember that the law of average says that if you play your best, you give yourself the best chance to win, but you are not guaranteed to win. As a peak performer, you cannot control the outcome; all you can do is work the process to the best of your ability and give yourself the best opportunity for performance success. The daily pursuit of excellence is the only way to get there.

THE EXCELLENCE OF BLUE ANGELS

Excellence is about preparing more than other people are willing to and working smarter than other people think is necessary. It is paying close attention to detail within the process in order to give you the results you desire. The Blue Angels are a group of United States Navy Fighter Pilots that perform aerial shows all over the country. What their audiences witness is excellence in motion. What the audience does not see is that entire performance process demands precision and a commitment to excellence before, and after, they take to the skies.

As some of the most dedicated and excellent performers on the planet, the Blue Angels use mental imagery, video analysis, and a routine brief and debriefing process each of which takes about twice as long as the flight itself. Known for their tight diamond formation in the air, where only 36 inches or one yard, separate the planes from the wingtip of one plane to the canopy of the other planes (36 inches is about how far your head is from your feet when you sit down and read this). They perform aerial maneuvers at a speed of one mile every 9 seconds or a closure rate, two planes flying directly towards each other, at one mile every 4 ½ seconds; almost 1,000 miles per hour. There is little to no room for error, and team excellence in their performance is critical.

PURSUIT OF EXCELLENCE OVER PERFECTION

The Blue Angels understand that their pursuit of excellence is different than the pursuit of perfection. They know that there has never been the perfect flight. They are constantly evaluating performance on video, looking for areas of improvement, paying close attention to the details of their flights, and even evaluating the way they march to their airplanes. The Blue Angels team is a model of excellence, and they are truly dedicated to progress and making the team better in their pursuit of excellence TODAY.

When you see the Blue Angels or other peak performers, like Michael Jordan or Georges St. Pierre, they make what they do look very easy and we think they are gifted. Do not be fooled by their grace and proficient performance. Although they may have been blessed with a few faster twitch muscle fibers than Joe Normal, even they have climbed The Mountain of Excellence one step at a time, and they would be the first to tell you so.

A WORLD CHAMPION STATE OF MIND

Whether you have the talent of a world champion, or not, is irrelevant. Physical skill makes these champions visibly impressive, but more important is their mental toughness. The story behind their physical prowess is the story of their mental prowess, because it is their incredible work ethic, their capacity to deflect adversity, and their insatiable desire to improve, to which they owe their success. One of the most beautiful aspects of the mental game is that, regardless of physical skill, you can become a master of it.

Most people believe that you must be great before you can practice like the great ones. Well, most people have got it all wrong. Anyone can create a program to cultivate the mindset of a champion. You may not lift the same amount of weight or run the same distance, but anyone can prepare and practice with the same mental intensity of a world champion. All physical performance programs should necessarily be tailored to the physical capabilities of the individual, but mental performance programs may be adopted universally. The fundamentals of mental conditioning may be practiced by anyone willing to actively pursue the summit of The Mountain of Excellence.

THE CLIMB IS THE DISCOVERY

As we have discussed throughout this manual, performance, in sport and in life, is comparable to that of a journey up a mountain. The journey is yours and you alone have the ability to set the tone of your performance to conquer the climb. The mountain you set your sights on is your choice and the journey is your discovery.

Each mountain you approach will require different physical skills that you must master, but the mental skill will remain the same. There will be some mountains that serve as pleasure climbs, while others will challenge your very existence by demanding every ounce of your physical and mental abilities. Sometimes, you will be climbing a mountain and you will realize you no longer wish to reach the summit. Sometimes, you will need to return to base camp, take a break, and return to conquer the summit at a later date. Each journey up a mountain is a journey of self-discovery, and through each experience, you learn a little about yourself and you learn a little bit about the journey. At the end of the day, the journey makes reaching the summit worthwhile.

THE JOURNEY IS THE REWARD, THE DESTINATION IS THE DISEASE

My hope is that by the end of this manual I will have taught you how to be an independent, peak performance mountaineer who understands that although you may reach the summit of the mountain you are climbing, there is no summit in life and there is no summit to your excellence. You are on a journey in which the journey is the reward and the destination is the disease. You must understand that every climb is a process and the proper preparation is imperative. You must create a mental road map, detailing where you want to go and who you want to become from a peak performance perspective. This will give you the best chance to reach the summit of that mountain. Once you reach it and have thoroughly enjoyed the view, it is time to return to base camp and start climbing another.

CAIN'S COACHING POINT:
There is always another mountain to climb, and throughout your journeys up the Mountains of Excellence, recognize there is no final summit; there is no finish line. You are on a journey called life and your best bet is to DOMINATE THE DAY, every day.

SUCCESS - THE RESULT OF EXCELLENCE

I have said this before and I will repeat myself for emphasis. *There is no shortcut to performance excellence, there is no easy way to the summit of your mountain.* Excellence is something you cannot purchase or be gifted, just as success is not something you simply randomly discover. Excellence is the result of a self-transformative journey that you choose to actively endure, and once you develop a strict adherence to personal excellence, you are bound to discover the success you are looking for.

THE MENTAL CONDITIONS FOR EXCELLENCE

Through the Mental Conditioning Manual: PRIDE Program, you have learned many mental conditioning strategies and peak performance principles to help you proceed on your journey to the summit of The Mountain of Excellence. Regardless of your sport or profession, the utilization of these mental conditioning principles and fundamentals are necessary to help achieve an elite and excellent performance state of mind.

At the conclusion of going through the Mental Conditioning Manual, you have learned how to:

- Live in the present moment and maximize your time.

- Act differently than how you feel and start having good bad days.

- Focus on the process over the outcome.

- Identify what you can control and what you cannot.

- Have your own personal philosophy and core values for life.

- Challenge your limiting beliefs and your perspective.

- Stay positive in the face of adversity.

- Develop preparation and performance routines for a consistently high-level performance.

- Take responsibility for your performance and life.

- Relax, recover, and gain control of your thoughts, feelings and emotions.

- Recognize your signal lights and develop the awareness to win.

- Release negative thoughts and refocus back to the present when you get distracted.

- Move from intelligence and thinking to action and results.

- Use mental imagery to help you prepare and be more confident in your performance.

- Inspire and motivate yourself to make the impossible possible.

- Develop the dedication and self-discipline that you need to power through the grind it takes to succeed.

- Take action steps to make excellence a lifestyle, not an event.

Remember, you will reach the summit of The Mountain of Excellence by focusing on the next 200 feet. When you take Personal Responsibility In Daily Excellence, everything else will take care of itself. Today, sign your name with excellence on everything and everyone you touch, and I will see you at the summit.

_____

YOUR SIGNATURE HERE   *DATE*

In Excellence, Your Mental Conditioning Coach

Brian Cain

CHAPTER #17 REVIEW

- Excellence is being at your best when it means the most – every single day.

- Excellence is a lifestyle; not an event.

- You have three doors you can choose to open. You can open the door called WIN, you can open the door called LOSE, or you can open the door called EXCELLENCE.

- Excellence is about preparing more than other people are willing to, and working smarter than other people think is necessary.

- The pursuit of excellence is constructive; the pursuit of perfection will destroy you.

- Anyone can develop a world champion state of mind.

- The journey makes reaching the summit worthwhile.

- The journey is the reward and the destination is the disease.

- Success is the result of excellence.

- When you take PRIDE (Personal Responsibility In Daily Excellence) in your performance, everything else will take care of itself.

- DOMINATE THE DAY!

NOTES:

NOTES:

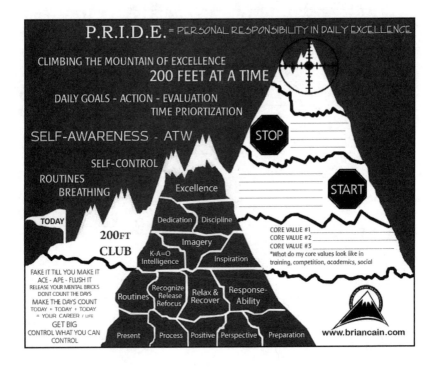

CHAPTER #18

What you want to do once you have completed *The Mental Conditioning Manual* is to set goals for yourself around the development of your peak performance mindset. The best way to do this is to follow the three steps for performance improvement taught to me by Harvey Dorfman and first mentioned in Chapter 1.

1. Develop an awareness of what needs to change.

2. Develop a strategy for change.

3. Implement the strategy with an accountability partner and assess regularly so that change can occur.

Most athletes fall short of significant performance improvement because they lack the awareness of what it is they need to change. Without such awareness, an athlete can never formulate an effective strategy that will facilitate the necessary change.

You must ask yourself, what do you want to change, why do you want to change, what are your goals for personal development? Remember, **to win a championship you must first become a champion.** The journey to becoming a champion starts when you start working on yourself.

To best work on yourself I suggest you create a 10-goal personal development plan and assessment that you share with an accountability partner and review each night before you go to bed with a short nightly assessment and formally assess 1-10 each Wednesday. After five weeks you will have a score between 5-50 for each of your goals. If you are between 40-50 in your self-assessment it is a good indicator that you have made significant personal development towards that goal and should create a new goal for your personal development. If you are under 40, you should spend another five weeks working at that goal and increasing your level of commitment.

I have shared with you an example of a personal development plan I use with the coaches, athletes and teams I work wtih. Although these specific goals may be different than yours, the process you will follow on your journey will be the same.

 You can download this sample personal development plan at www.MentalConditioningManual.com/extras so that you do not have to recreate the wheel. Just refine it and customize it for your personal development.

DOMINATE THE DAY!

Brian Cain Peak Performance, LLC
Mental Conditioning & Personal Development Plan (PDP)

Personal Plan For Jon Doe
Accountability Partner – Brian Cain
Assessment Period (5 WEEKS 8/8/2012 – 9/5/2012)
Nightly Assessment - Round 1 – Assessment 1 – 8/8/2012

"You Treasure What You Measure" & *"Measurement = Motivation"*
"Awareness Is The First Step Towards Accomplishment"

This assessment is designed to help you learn about the progress you have made on executing your personal mental conditioning and personal development plan. Please write in your scores from each of the past five weeks.

PERSONAL DEVELOPMENT PLAN NIGHTLY ASSESSMENT	W	T	F	S	S	M	T
1. I go to bed and wake up at consistent times and get 8-9:15 hours of sleep							
2. I drink 2/3 of my body weight in fluid OZ of water every day							
3. I do mental imagery three times a week before bed on Mon, Wed, Thurs							
4. I meditate/relaxation twice a day for a 10 Breath inhale of 6-8 and exhale of 8-10							
5. I use a daily planner to help me stay organized with my time							
6. I love what I do, smile & enjoy the grind and the journey, no pressure/all pleasure							
7. I stay organized, touch it once, never e-mail graze & use systems to be efficient							
8. I make it about others, I engage, ask questions & listen intently w/o interruption							
9. I exercise for at least 30 minutes every day, health and fitness is a lifestyle for me							
10. I focus on what I can control and let go of what I cannot control							

I am to put this nightly check sheet somewhere that I can see it as a part of my nightly routine before I go to bed and will assess myself each night on my progress that day at DOMINATING my personal development plan. This should take only 1-2 minutes per night and will only be accomplished if it is built into my nightly routine. I will also jot notes that will help remind me of what I want to do to keep taking steps towards excellence and the DOMINATION of my personal development plan.

Brian Cain Peak Performance, LLC
Mental Conditioning & Personal Development Plan (PDP)

Personal Plan For Jon Doe
Accountability Partner – Brian Cain
Assessment Period (5 WEEKS 8/8/2012 – 9/5/2012)
Weekly Assessment - Round 1 – Assessment 1 – 8/8/2012

"You Treasure What You Measure" & *"Measurement = Motivation"*
"Awareness Is The First Step Towards Accomplishment"

This assessment is designed to help you learn about the progress you have made on executing your personal mental conditioning and personal development plan. Please write in your scores from each of the past five weeks.

PERSONAL DEVELOPMENT PLAN NIGHTLY ASSESSMENT	SD D U A SA
1. I go to bed and wake up at consistent times and get 8-9:15 hours of sleep	1 2 3 4 5 6 7 8 9 10
2. I drink 2/3 of my body weight in fluid OZ of water every day	1 2 3 4 5 6 7 8 9 10
3. I do mental imagery three times a week before bed on Mon, Wed, Thurs	1 2 3 4 5 6 7 8 9 10
4. I meditate/relaxation twice a day for a 10 Breath inhale of 6-8 and exhale of 8-10	1 2 3 4 5 6 7 8 9 10
5. I use a daily planner to help me stay organized with my time	1 2 3 4 5 6 7 8 9 10
6. I love what I do, smile & enjoy the grind and the journey, no pressure/all pleasure	1 2 3 4 5 6 7 8 9 10
7. I stay organized, touch it once, never e-mail graze & use systems to be efficient	1 2 3 4 5 6 7 8 9 10
8. I make it about others, I engage, ask questions & listen intently w/o interruption	1 2 3 4 5 6 7 8 9 10
9. I exercise for at least 30 minutes every day, health and fitness is a lifestyle for me	1 2 3 4 5 6 7 8 9 10
10. I focus on what I can control and let go of what I cannot control	1 2 3 4 5 6 7 8 9 10
2 = Strongly Disagree 4 = Disagree 6 = Undecided 8= Agree 10 = Strongly Agree	Total _____/100

SCORE	RATING	COMMENTS
90-100	Excellent	I am following my PDP extremely closely and am seeing the benefits from my work.
80-89	Great	Overall I'm doing well at following my PDP; a few improvements should help.
70-79	Good	I'm doing OK with following my PDP; I need to make key commitments to improve.
60-69	Okay	I am struggling with my PDP and need to recommit with my accountability partner.
50-59	Poor	I am beating myself badly and need to get my head back into the game. I have serious work to do.
0-49	Chaos	I need to start over and redefine who I want to become and make significant life changes.

WRITTEN PERFORMANCE BREAK-DOWN OF MY ASSESSMENT ABOVE:

Written assessment of my evaluation and what I have learned:_____

_____

_____

_____

_____

_____

_____

Two things I will START doing to improve my performance:

1) _____

2) _____

Two things I will STOP doing to improve my performance:

1) _____

2) _____

Two things I will CONTINUE doing to improve my performance:

1) _____

2) _____

Brian Cain Peak Performance, LLC
Mental Conditioning & Personal Development Plan (PDP)

Personal Plan For Jon Doe
Accountability Partner – Brian Cain
Assessment Period (5 WEEKS 8/8/2012 – 9/5/2012)
5 Week Assessment Total Tally Sheet - Round 1
Final Assessment – 9/5/2012

"You Treasure What You Measure" & *"Measurement = Motivation"*
"Awareness Is The First Step Towards Accomplishment"

This assessment is designed to help you learn about the progress you have made on executing your personal mental conditioning and personal development plan. Please write in your scores from each of the past five weeks.

PERSONAL DEVELOPMENT PLAN
5 WEEK TALLY SHEET

1. I go to bed and wake up at consistent times and get 8-9:15 hours of sleep	1_ 2_ 3_ 4_ 5_ TOT__
2. I drink 2/3 of my body weight in fluid OZ of water every day	1_ 2_ 3_ 4_ 5_ TOT__
3. I do mental imagery three times a week before bed on Mon, Wed, Thurs	1_ 2_ 3_ 4_ 5_ TOT__
4. I meditate/relaxation twice a day for a 10 Breath inhale of 6-8 and exhale of 8-10	1_ 2_ 3_ 4_ 5_ TOT__
5. I use a daily planner to help me stay organized with my time	1_ 2_ 3_ 4_ 5_ TOT__
6. I love what I do, smile & enjoy the grind and the journey, no pressure/all pleasure	1_ 2_ 3_ 4_ 5_ TOT__
7. I stay organized, touch it once, never e-mail graze & use systems to be efficient	1_ 2_ 3_ 4_ 5_ TOT__
8. I make it about others, I engage, ask questions & listen intently w/o interruption	1_ 2_ 3_ 4_ 5_ TOT__
9. I exercise for at least 30 minutes every day, health and fitness is a lifestyle for me	1_ 2_ 3_ 4_ 5_ TOT__
10. I focus on what I can control and let go of what I cannot control	1_ 2_ 3_ 4_ 5_ TOT__

SCORE	RATING	COMMENTS
40-50	Excellent	I am following my PDP extremely close and am seeing the benefits from my work.
30-39	Great	Overall I'm doing well at following my PDP; a few improvements should help.
20-29	Good	I'm doing OK with following my PDP; I need to make key commitments to improve.
10-19	Okay	I am struggling with my PDP and need to recommit with my accountability partner.
0-09	Poor	I am beating myself badly and need to get my head back into the game. I have serious work to do.

When you add up the five assessments of your ROUND 1 PERSONAL DEVELOPMENT PLAN, if you are between 40-50, that is a positive lifestyle change and characteristic and you can remove that goal and select a new goal off of the program Core Values sheet or you can create a new goal that is specific and custom for you that when it becomes a lifestyle, you will improve your chances for success.

When writing your new goals, be sure that you write them in the present tense, process based and positively. By putting your goals on the personal development plan you are making a commitment to becoming that person NOW!

It is critical that you get feedback from your coaches, teammates and accountability partner about what you can do and who you need to become to give yourself the best chance for success to reach the summit of The Mountain of Excellence.

 If you are interested in having me or a member of my team work with you personally as your accountability partner, please visit www.BrianCain.com/accountability and fill out the Accountability Partner Request form and a member of Brian Cain Peak Performance will follow up with you.

Thank you for honoring me with your most valuable asset, your time. I look forward to working with you on your journey to the summit of The Mountain of Excellence and helping you to DOMINATE THE DAY!

In Excellence, Your Mental Conditioning Coach

CAIN'S COACHING POINT:

If you have found value in using this manual and if it has helped you in anyway, consider giving a copy to five people whom you care about and want to see take their performance to the next level. By giving them this manual, you are helping me, but more importantly you are helping someone else find the ideas and mental keys that will unlock their potential. You will help them live a more fulfilled and excellent journey as they climb Their Mountain of Excellence. This manual could forever alter the course of someone's life. It could be you who provides the push. Without you, they might never even start hiking.

Write down five people to whom you will give a copy of this manual:

1) _____

2) _____

3) _____

4) _____

5) _____

ABOUT THE AUTHOR

WHO IS BRIAN CAIN?

Brian M. Cain, MS, CMAA, is a #1 Best Selling Author, speaker, trainer and expert in the fields of Mental Conditioning and Peak Performance. He has worked with coaches, athletes, and teams at the Olympic level and in the National Football League (NFL), National Basketball Association (NBA), National Hockey League (NHL), Ultimate Fighting Championship (UFC), and Major League Baseball (MLB).

Cain has also worked with programs in some of the top college athletic departments around the country including the University of Alabama, Auburn University, Florida State University, the University of Iowa, the University of Maryland, the University of Mississippi, Mississippi State University, Oregon State University, the University of Southern California, the University of Tennessee, Vanderbilt University, Washington State University, Yale University, Texas A & M, TCU, Baylor, the University of Georgia, the University of Vermont and many others.

Cain has worked as a mental-conditioning consultant with numerous high school, state, and national championship programs. He has delivered his award-winning seminars and presentations at coaches' clinics, leadership summits, and athletic directors' conventions all over the country. As a high-school athletic director, he is one of the youngest ever to receive the Certified Master Athletic Administration Certification from the National Interscholastic Athletic Administrators Association.

A highly-sought-after Peak Performance Coach, clinician, and keynote and motivational speaker, Cain delivers his message with passion, enthusiasm, and in an engaging style that keeps his audiences entertained while being educated. As someone who lives what he teaches, Cain will inspire you and give you the tools necessary to get the most out of your career.

 Find out when Cain will be coming to your area by visiting his calendar at www.briancain.com/calendar.

WHERE'S CAIN?

Cain's Calendar:

"I want to book Cain when he's in town."

RESOURCES GUIDE

HOW CAN YOU BECOME A MASTER OF THE MENTAL GAME: FIND OUT WHAT THE INNER CIRCLE DELIVERS

If you are a serious coach or athlete looking to take your performance to another level, I highly encourage you to join the Brian Cain Peak Performance Inner Circle. Members receive interviews with top coaches and athletes, videos of top performance routines, and inside access to Cain and his teachings. The Brian Cain Peak Performance Inner Circle will help you play at your best when it means the most.

Log-on to www.briancaininnercircle.com to sign up today.

THE PRIDE PEAK PERFORMANCE SYSTEM

PRIDE – PERSONAL RESPONSIBILITY IN DAILY EXCELLENCE

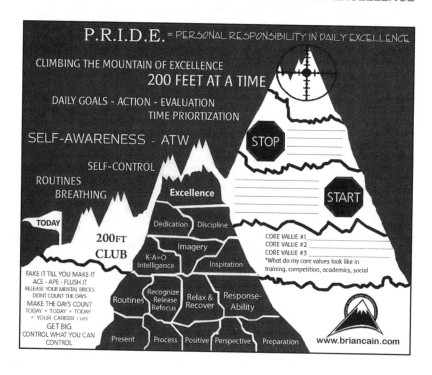

Have You or Your Team Ever Struggled With...

- Working hard physically *but still not getting the results you deserve?*

- Creating a system to *teach character and toughness* that translates to the field?

- *Investing time and money into books, videos and programs* that do not yield results?

- Repeatedly *getting it done in practice, but failing to do so when the lights come on?*

- *Choking in pressure situations* time after time, even though you have been there before?

The PRIDE Peak-Performance System Will...

- Give you the best step-by-step system ever created for developing mental toughness.

- Teach you the same mental-toughness system used by world-champion athletes.

- Be the equivalent of having the *world's best strength and conditioning coach... for your brain.*

- Positively *change your athletic and coaching career.*

- *Unlock your potential* and teach you how to be your best every day.

Cain's Peak Performance System (PRIDE – Personal Responsibility In Daily Excellence) is a six-DVD Peak Performance training program featuring eighteen 10-25 minute videos and a 100+ page manual designed for the coach or athlete looking to gain a competitive advantage. From Peak-Performance and Mental-Toughness Training, Cain goes in-depth on the following topics:

1. The Language of Mental Toughness

2. 200FT Club & Core Covenants

3. Present-Moment Focus

4. Process-Over-Outcome Approaches

5. Championship Perspective

6. Positive Mental Attitudes

7. Preparation Routines for Confidence

8. Preparation Routines for Consistent Performance

9. RESPONSE-Ability Training

10. In-depth Relaxation & Recovery Training

11. Performance-Awareness Development

12. K-A=O – The Intelligence Factor

13. Mental-Imagery Training

14. Inspiration & Motivation that Works

15. Dedication & Commitment

16. Discipline as a Positive Life Skill

17. Excellence as a Lifestyle, Not an Event

18. Interview with an MMA World Champion

 Visit www.briancain.com/cainproducts/pride
For A Sneak Peak of The PRIDE Peak
Performance system in action.

THE PEAK PERFORMANCE BOOTCAMP

CAIN'S LIVE FOUR-HOUR SEMINAR

2 DVDS, 3 AUDIO CDS, MANUAL

Have You or Your Team Ever Struggled With...

- The ability to *sustain consistently high levels of performance?*

- *Getting distracted* by a large crowd, hostile environment or "BIG GAME?"

- Finding ways to keep your team *motivated to work HARD & SMART everyday?*

- Ways to *make practice more competitive* and intense?

- *Choking in pressure situations* time after time even though you have been there before?

Today You Can Discover How To Help Your Team:

- Gain the mental toughness they need to *out-play and out-perform* even the toughest competition.

- *Play in the moment* and destroy all those mental blocks that kill performance.

- Take control over the speed and the flow of the game so all the competition is *playing at your pace.*

- Shatter their beliefs about what they "cannot do."

- Give them the tools *to accomplish things they once only dreamed of.*

- Develop the *team chemistry* you need to bring home a championship.

 For A Sneak Peak of The PRIDE Peak Performance Bootcamp visit www.briancain.com/cainproducts/bootcamp

INTRODUCTION TO PEAK PERFORMANCE AUDIO PROGRAM

WELCOME TO MENTAL TOUGHNESS TRAINING

Have You or Your Team Ever Struggled With...

- Consistently *playing at your best?*

- Finding the motivation it takes to *work hard every day?*

- Maintaining *confidence* when you are *not playing well?*

- Choking in pressure situations *time after time* even though you have been there before?

The Introduction To Peak Performance CD Will...

- Give you insight into the *fundamentals of peak performance.*

- Help you to become a *Master of The Mental Game.*

- Increase your *ability to overcome adversity.*

- Teach you the psychological skills necessary to *perform consistently at your best.*

"This CD lives in my car's CD player. Cain breaks down the fundamental aspects of mental toughness and gives you the skills necessary to teach toughness to your team. Every coach and athlete should have this CD in their car or on their iPod at all times."

Erik Bakich
Head Baseball Coach
University of Michigan

At the elite levels, athletic performance is 90% mental and 10% physical.

In this CD you get the information you need to perform your best when it means the most.

You get the tactics, the training, and the secrets you need to increase your mental toughness.

You get the tools that will put your mental game MILES AHEAD of every other athlete and team in your league, in your conference, or in your division.

That is exactly why I created this CD... so that YOU can discover:

- Why sport psychology and *peak performance are crucial* to your success this season!

- The tricks and methods that teach you how to *let go of the things you cannot control* during play!

- The *3 "magic letters"* that turn statements of failure into goal-setting exclamations!

- How to make *excellence a LIFESTYLE* and not a once-in-a-while event!

- The little secrets that allow you to *increase your ability to play at a quicker tempo!*

- The right way – *and the wrong way – to talk on defense!*

"I started using this CD when I met Cain and it has helped me be a better fighter, a better coach, more mentally tough, and more confident. Learning to focus on the things I can control, learning that confidence is a choice, learning not to count the days but to make the days count has had a tremendous impact on my career. Cain covers all of this and his P.R.I.D.E. program in this CD. I cannot recommend this CD any more highly to the coach or athlete looking to increase his performance with mental toughness training."

Rob MacDonald
Professional Mixed Martial Arts Fighter, UFC
Strength and Conditioning Coach, Gym Jones

 Visit www.BrianCain.com/products for more information

TOILETS, BRICKS, FISH HOOKS AND PRIDE:

THE PEAK PERFORMANCE TOOLBOX EXPOSED

CAIN'S #1 BEST SELLING BOOK

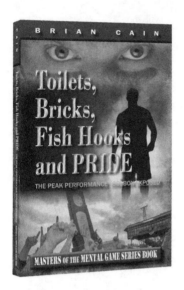

Featured on ESPN

Have you ever experienced any of the following?

- Continually *falling short of your potential?*
- *Mental game breakdowns* under pressure?
- Coaches or athletes who simply are *not as motivated as you?*
- Wasting time thinking about things you have *no control over?*
- *Losing to an inferior opponent* more than once in a season
- Wanting to quit because you *lost the love?*
- Coaches that make a simple sport *more complex than it needs to be?*

 Visit www.ToiletsBricksFishHooksandPride.com For FREE Extras, Updates & Information

SO WHAT, NEXT PITCH!

*HOW TO PLAY YOUR BEST
WHEN IT MEANS THE MOST*

BOOK TWO IN THE SERIES

SO WHAT, NEXT PITCH! WILL:

- Give you a system for playing the game one pitch at a time

- Take you inside some of the best minds in the game of baseball

- Show you how to deal with failure both on the field and in life

- Serve as your map on the journey to mental toughness

- Unlock your potential and give you the mental keys to success

"This book will make a difference in the way you compete in baseball, but more importantly, the way you compete at the game of life."

Dave Serrano, Head Baseball Coach
The University of Tennessee

"Moving on to the next pitch is easier said than done. This book will show you how to do it."

Gary Gilmore, Head Baseball Coach
Coastal Carolina University
2012 Big South Conference Champions
& 2012 Big South Coach of The Year

"So What, Next Pitch! It is something that you hear all the time in baseball. In this book you learn some strategies that will help you play the game one pitch at a time and overcome the failure that is part of the game."

Trevor Moawad, MAT, Director of Performance
IMG Academies

 Visit www.SoWhatNextPitch.com For BONUS Mental Conditioning Material & Peak Performance Training Tools

CONNECT WITH CAIN
THROUGH SOCIAL MEDIA

YOUR LINK TO DOING A LITTLE A LOT, NOT A LOT A LITTLE

 www.twitter.com/briancainpeak

 www.facebook.com/briancainpeak

 www.linkedin.com/briancainpeak

 www.youtube.com/wwwbriancaincom

 www.briancain.com/itunes

SIGN UP FOR YOUR FREE NEWSLETTER
www.BrianCain.com

NOTES:

NOTES: